~500

D1106533

MOHOLY-NAGY:

Photographs and Photograms

MOHOLY-NAGY:

Photographs and Photograms

by **Andreas Haus**

translation from the German
by Frederic Samson

Pantheon Books
New York

Library of Congress Cataloging in Publication Data

Moholy-Nagy, László, 1895–1946
   Moholy-Nagy, photographs and photograms
   Translation of Moholy-Nagy, Fotos und Fotogramme
Bibliography – p.
   1.   Photography, Artistic.   2.   Photograms.
   3.   Moholy-Nagy, László, 1895–1946.
      I. Haus, Andreas.   II. Title
TR 654.M6213   770'.92'4   79–1880
ISBN 0–394–50449–6

Manufactured in West Germany

FIRST AMERICAN EDITION

CONTENTS

PREFACE

Moholy's historical role, taken together with his own singular intellectual range and versatility, is such that any analytical approach to his œuvre must be not only a study in depth, but one that is sweeping enough to include research into the results of his work in the most varied artistic media, as well as following numerous international trails.

Many pictures and creations in different spheres, some of them published for the first time in this volume, would not have come to my notice without the willing and not infrequently unexpected help and support of numerous individuals and institutions. I therefore wish to thank all those whose assistance has played a part in the preparation of this book, including the relatives of László Moholy-Nagy: Frau Lucia Moholy of Zurich, for invaluable information; also Frau Hattula Hug-Moholy-Nagy, of Zurich, for her active interest in dealing with all kinds of questions. Others whom I must include are: Dr H. H. Klihm, Munich; the Director and staff of the Bauhaus-Archiv, Berlin; Dr Hannah Steckel-Weitemeier, Berlin; and Dr Carola Giedion-Welcker, Zurich. Likewise, helpful information was supplied by Dr László Beke, Budapest; Dr Janos Brendel, Warsaw; Anna Gara-Bak, Berlin; Dr Juliane Roh, Munich; Professor Max Bill, Zurich; Professor Herbert Bayer, Aspen, Col.; Professor Beaumont Newhall; Professor L. Fritz-Gruber; Helmut Gernsheim; and Dr Karl Jacob-Steinorth.

Institutions and individuals to whom acknowledgment is due include: in Berlin, the Kunstbibliothek of the Staatliche Museen Stiftung Preußischer Kulturbesitz, as well as the Landesbildstelle, for facilities for studying original sources; in Budapest, the Society of Hungarian Photographic Artists, for friendly co-operation; in Rochester, N.Y., the International Museum of Photography, especially Christine Hawrylak, Michael Kamins and Dr Ulrich Keller; Susan Kismaric at the Museum of Modern Art, New York; David Travis at the Art Institute of Chicago (Levy Collection); David W. Steadman at Pomona College, Claremont, Cal.; Joe Coltharp at the Gernsheim Collection, University of Texas, Austin; Peter Obermüller at the Kunstgewerbemuseum, Zurich; Donald B. Goodall at the University of Texas, Austin; and William Larson, Philadelphia.

Numerous others have alleviated the burden of my work by providing originals for reproduction and by kindly furnishing information; to all of these I extend heartfelt thanks, as well as to all those who helped in the preparation of the book itself.

Marburg/Lahn, March 1978   Andreas Haus

METHODICAL INTRODUCTION TO THE PROBLEM :
a painter makes photographic history

This book is the first monograph on László Moholy-Nagy as a photographer. Connoisseurs of the history of photography may be surprised to learn that such a monograph had not appeared much earlier, for the relevant literature long ago accorded the photographer Moholy a prominent place in the ranks of the avant-garde, i.e. those who in the 1920s had begun consciously to make use for the first time of optical-technical laws specific to photographic procedure as an 'elementary' means for the composition of pictures.

Thus, *From Hill to Moholy-Nagy* and *Photography from its Beginnings to Moholy*[1] are examples of titles of photo-historical exhibitions and treatises in which Moholy's name stands as a decisive landmark and turning point in the historical development of photography. Before Moholy we find the photographic reproduction of reality making use of atmospheric devices borrowed from painting. With Moholy, and after him, 'creative' photography comes into existence, with its shift of interest to such abstract factors as light, shadow, perspective and structure.

Moholy is given credit for two decisive innovations: (1) the concept of the 'New Vision', i.e. an education for visual experiences of a new kind with the aid of perspectives and optical angles made possible by the camera; (2) the photogram ('Fotogramm') which, without the aid of a camera and merely by a chemical process of building up tones through exposure to light, developed abstract pictorial compositions on sensitized paper.

Moholy's motto was 'Fotografie ist Lichtgestaltung'[2] (photography is manipulation of light). In the name of this motto he reduced all the graphic and concrete qualities of photography to the medium of light, which is basic to the photographic process, and demanded from the photographer that he should regard as his main task the systematic examination and application of light. In thus defining the creative act not by its meaning and purpose but by its means, he could claim for photography its own competence

as a plastic manipulation of light, just as painting was a plastic manipulation of colours, architecture a plastic manipulation of space, and sculpture a plastic manipulation of mass. Seemingly this was an ingenious stroke with which to decide, on purely functional grounds, the debate as to whether or not photography was an art. But Moholy went even further: he accorded to *light* such an absolute priority as an element of composition that he claimed all other elements such as mass, space and colour to be dependent on it.

However, it is evident that, notwithstanding all this, Moholy did not see photography as a law unto itself, as just 'itself', but that he regarded it as having a more general significance. He saw in it 'the' technique which permitted the photographer to 'manipulate' light in varying degrees of differentiation and purity as the supreme and most general element of the plastic arts — something that painting by its use of brush and pigment had hitherto never achieved. As a matter of fact Moholy never called himself a photographer. The rather strange new word *Lichtner*[3] (manipulator of light) is a self-coined expression for what Moholy always was: a painter. However 'multimedial' his activities were, whether as graphic artist, typographer, photographer, arranger of exhibitions, designer, film maker, teacher and writer, Moholy always described himself as a painter.[4] It was as a painter that he had raised photography to the status of an art, but exclusively in the sense that he reconstructed it as a new painting technique. As an artist Moholy was a painter, as a photographer he was a dilettante in the full sense of the word: the newly discovered techniques fired him with a genuine zeal for experimentation, filling him with a theoretician's missionary urge of astonishing intensity.

From this point of view a description of Moholy as a photographer is more problematical than it appeared at the outset, for both author and reader are given the task of seeing the artist not merely in connection with photography but in a wider art-historical context. It will be necessary to undertake an extended excursion even into unknown regions of the history of art in the 1920s. A further problem arises from the fact that Moholy never quite attained the same distinction in a traditional field of art as was accorded him by the world of photography. Moholy the painter was never considered as particularly important in the historical development of painting. In exhibitions and museums his works rarely radiate the brilliance and intensity of a Lissitzky, Mondrian or Malevich. At times his painterly works make a strangely indistinct and theoretical impression. On the other hand, his photographs show inventiveness and liveliness and not infrequently spirit and a bizarre humour. Does such a discrepancy signify the victory of the dilettante over the professional? The varying powers of expression of artistic media represent the dialectic between realism and abstraction in human consciousness and lay bare a crisis in the relationship between the individual and his social environment.

During the last decade art-historical studies have exploded the dogma (which had become almost unshakable in the West) that the history of art was to end, with the inexorableness of a natural law, in pure abstraction. Pointing to the 'social relevance' of all art, realism was declared to be the sole basis for an art which could serve social understanding and progress. Recent photo-nostalgia and photo-theory are founded on the aspect of realism inherent in the medium of photography and are based on an understanding of the quality of 'social documentation'[5] in historical photographs.

For this reason the 'abstract' photography of a Moholy was long regarded as not being 'relevant' whilst the politically committed photography of the 1920s, photomontage and pictures of the working classes, attracted most attention. It was only a short time ago that a newly aroused enthusiasm for the photographic avant-garde of the 1920s caught the imagination of both the public and art dealers and led to a new theoretical look at this subject.

Thus the photography of the Bauhaus and of Neue Sachlichkeit (New Objectivity)[6] were considered for the first time in their relationship to the conditions of industrial production. It was said of 'new objective' advertising photography: 'Such pictures lend to objects a bizarre unexpected look and suggest that they have a life of their own, and one quite unexpected by the public. They are the modern still-lifes of the twentieth century, the expression of exchange value and of the detached fetish-like character of a commodity.'[7] Thus, for the first time, economic *function*[8] was also documented and a step taken beyond the 'reproduction of reality' in photography — the aspect which hitherto had been almost exclusively considered. A more comprehensive understanding of the powers of photography to mirror reality had been reached. However, in the last analysis, such a statement smacks too much of a denunciation and bars the way to a wider critical understanding of the images concerned.

The 'non-professional' photographer Moholy-Nagy cannot be linked with the known trends of the time — or only quite superficially. He certainly does not belong to Neue Sachlichkeit, and the idea of Bauhaus photography as such is hardly identifiable as a historical entity. The only category applicable to Moholy, that of Constructivism, if used as an absolute, would lead to a far-reaching misunderstanding of his photography. This is the real justification for treating Moholy as a 'photographer' despite all that has been said above, though it is necessary to view him in a broad historical context. His photography is more than simply different from his painting; it means more not only as regards the content of his statements but in the entire determination of this content.

Hence, to formulate a provisional thesis, one might say that Moholy's photographs are using and at the same time testing Constructivist theories of perception and composition as applied to reality. This results, almost automatically at times, in quite novel aesthetic insights which could not have been attained either through photography or through painting by themselves. One of the unexpected consequences of Moholy's naïve linking of theoretical and practical spheres is that he is thereby getting close to surrealist procedures, hardly definable in his work until then. The antecedents of this can only be partly explained by Moholy's close relationship with Dadaism. It is one of the aims of this book to show that these pseudo-realistic (or *überrealistisch* — 'over-realistic' — a term coined by Moholy)[9] achievements form, with their contradictions, the most fruitful areas in Moholy's creative work.

THE BEGINNING:
'Manifesto on Elemental Art' and 'Dynamic of the Metropolis', 1921/22

Moholy's earliest properly attested interest in the medium of photography stems from a sphere far removed from the Bauhaus. It derives from the Dadaist principle of montage and its endeavour to find forms of presentation that transcended Futurism. The meeting point of the Constructivists and Dadaists lay in the principle of the 'elementary'. Moholy's first art-historical commitment was his signing, together with Ivan Puni, Raoul Hausmann and Hans Arp, of the 'Aufruf zur Elementaren Kunst' ('Manifesto on Elemental Art'),[10] the text of which clearly bears the mark of a synthesis of Dadaism and Constructivism.

In 1920 Hausmann had written in No. 3 of *Dada*: 'DADA forms the world cleverly according to its own data; it employs all forms and usages to destroy the morally pharisaic world of the bourgeoisie with its own means . . . the Dadaist uses bluff to leap beyond his own greed for sensation and meaning.'

In 1921 all this suddenly became the *style*, under the influence of Theo van Doesburg's De Stijl. Dada had split up. Grosz, Heartfield and others had joined the German Communist Party and agitated in support of the working class. Hausmann had discovered Constructivism; he still fought the 'philistines', but now he did so with the theory of elemental art which he called 'Presentism'. Moholy-Nagy joined the remainder of the Berlin 'Dadaists' just at the moment when they turned away from an absolute rejection of the bourgeois environment and began to see not only decadence in the 'American' dynamic of the city but also a new stimulus that was a gain for the vitality of the avant-garde vis-à-vis a bourgeoisie paralyzed by its reactionary attitudes. The method was to destroy aesthetically the alienated complexity of the real moment of motion in order to gain from it elements for its sovereign presentation. The *material* was Dadaist, the *montage* Constructivist. The model for the montage principle was the cinema — which had also fascinated the Futurists. They, however, had contented themselves with faceting the bubbling continuum into a shimmering mass whilst the Dadaists isolated single facts and produced dialectical contrasts. The Futurists operated with the physiological effects of moving images, the Dadaists with the psychological effects — akin to cinematic cutting techniques — on the aesthetic idea; and this transition from 'perception' to 'cognition' opened up at the same time new possibilities for 'manipulation'

AUFRUF ZUR ELEMENTAREN KUNST

An die Künstler der Welt!

Wir lieben die kühne Erfindung, die Erneuerung in der Kunst. Die Kunst, das ist die Konsequenz all der Kräfte einer Zeit. Wir leben in der Gegenwart. Und so fordern wir die Konsequenz unserer Zeit, eine Kunst, die nur von uns ausgehen kann, die es nicht vor uns gab und nicht nach uns geben wird — nicht wie eine wechselnde Mode, sondern aus der Erkenntnis, daß die Kunst ewig neu ist und nicht bei den Konsequenzen der Vergangenheit halt macht. Wir treten für die elementare Kunst ein. Elementar ist die Kunst, weil sie nicht philosophiert, weil sie sich aufbaut aus den ihr allein eigenen Elementen. Den Elementen der Gestaltung nachgeben, heißt Künstler sein. Die Elemente der Kunst können nur vom Künstler gefunden werden. Sie entstehen nicht aus seiner individuellen Willkür; das Individuum ist keine Absonderung und der Künstler ist nur ein Exponent der Kräfte, die die Elemente der Welt zur Gestalt bringen. Künstler, erklärt Euch solidarisch mit der Kunst! — Wendet Euch ab von den Stilen. Wir fordern die Stillosigkeit um zum **Stil** zu gelangen! Der Stil ist niemals das Plagiat!

Dieses Manifest gilt uns als Tat: Erfaßt von der Bewegung unserer Zeit verkünden wir mit der elementaren Kunst die Erneuerung unserer Anschauung, unseres Bewußtseins von den sich unermüdlich kreuzenden Kraftquellen, die den Geist und die Form einer Epoche bilden und in ihr die Kunst als etwas Reines, von der Nützlichkeit und der Schönheit Befreites, als etwas Elementares im Individuum entstehen lassen.

Wir fordern die elementare Kunst! gegen die Reaktion in der Kunst!   Berlin, Okt. 1921

R. Hausmann, Hans Arp, Iwan Puni, Maholy-Nagy

Fig. 1 The original manifesto on 'elemental art' (for translation see Appendix, p. 46).

(*Gestaltung*). At the first Dada Fair in Berlin in 1921 there was on exhibition a collage by Grosz and Heartfield (also used as the catalogue cover illustration) called 'Leben und Treiben in Universal City' ('Life and goings-on in Universal City').[11] A loudspeaker intoned the word 'Photoplays' and was aided by a film strip and other pointers to the cinema. At that exhibition Hausmann showed a collage 'Dada-Cino' ('Dada-Cinema'). He had already written in 1918 on the 'Synthetic Cinema of Painting', saying: 'Dada is the perfect form of friendly maliciousness; it is, next to photographic precision, the only justifiable pictorial form of communication and of balance in common experience — everyone who has within himself his own tendency towards salvation is a Dadaist. In Dada you will recognize your real state: wonderful constellations in real material, wire, glass, cardboard, fabric, organically corresponding to your own personality, complete with its cracks and bruises.'[12] Photography, then, is viewed as a piece of 'material' reality which, together with other 'elements', is to produce in montage a dynamic cinematic effect: 'L'Art Dada offers you immense stimulation, an impulse to acquire the real experience of all relationships . . . it produces relationships which only we, through our wonderful organisms full of contradictions, are able to assist in becoming justified, a rotating middle axis, a reason for standing or falling.'[13] According to Hausmann, only the 'elementary' equality of Subject-perception and Object-qualities could bring about a situation in which man felt himself to be at the centre of all relationships in a world in motion and the self-motivated agent of the 'synthesis'. In this way the static ideal of harmony in bourgeois aesthetics was redefined and activated into the changeable function of the material dialectic.

When, in 1921, Hausmann published his *Présentismus – gegen den Puffkeismus der teutschen Seele* ('Presentism – against the philistinism of the Germanic soul'), this materialist element appeared to be already strangely sublimated, however. 'We do not want the light which penetrates all bodies, or its subtle emanations rich in relationships, to disappear before our very eyes . . . In this central European shallowness we want to see at long last the aspect of a world which is real, which is a synthesis of spirit and matter.'[14] The dialectic aspect of montage seems almost to have been transformed into a new overall-kinetic state. 'We want to be hurled around and torn asunder by the mysterious dimension, our sixth sense,

motion. In this way we may be conscious of living, of living today! And so we want, first of all, to dissolve the rigidly concentrated look at one thing, because we have received historically into our way of seeing all optical possibilities and we now progress in optics to the fundamental phenomena of light. We love light and its motion . . .'[15]

In Moholy's sketch for a filmscript *Dynamic of the Metropolis* of 1921/22[16] all these maxims from aesthetic theory seem to be put into practice: the simultaneous character of montage can be found in a cutting process producing bizarre contrasts; the 'hurling' motion in distorted perspectives and the rotating camera; the sublimation of motion to light phenomena in shots of streets taken at night and in illuminated signs. All these attainments will have to be discussed further. At this point it is important, above all, to keep in mind that the basic sensual experience which underlies Moholy's filmscript is not the Constructivist aspect of technology but his lively individual perception of traffic in a metropolis. A more exact analysis of Moholy's script should demonstrate how very imaginatively he cut from the category of industrial 'production' to the dynamics of 'circulation' (at the very start of the film there appear pictures of a zeppelin and a house being built). Moholy, the artist here, shows himself more sensitive and more 'realistic' than Moholy the theoretician who, for the most part, talked rather indiscriminately of *machines* and *technology*, whilst the artist reproduced intuitively and without naming it the forceful and alien power exercized by the pressure of economic considerations. The theme of Moholy's script is, above all, an analysis of human needs for natural perception and communication in their struggle against the automatism of traffic in a modern metropolis (the difficulties of making a 'phone call, the glassy looks, the mechanical greetings, the twitching heads etc.). People appear to be strangely misdirected by the power of an ever-invoked *tempo* (e.g. people being hurled around on the Big Dipper). Tempo appears in the shape of military marches and mechanically operated performers. Scattered throughout are images of menaced and menacing nature: a tiger in its cage, an angry lynx, lions, a circus elephant, a slaughterhouse with raging cattle, and finally a dead chicken. Greed, in the shape of the profitable use of everything by modern production, is hinted at by showing how the rubbish of the metropolis is recycled, in a continuous process, back into the factories. Last, but not least, the reification of political domination is revealed by means of cutting from a shot of the police on the Potsdamer Platz in Berlin to a blow-up of a police truncheon, followed by the confrontation of a laughing theatre audience with the wide-open jaws of a lion. This sequence contains a clear pointer to Moholy's 'formalistic' insight into the blocking of understanding by the appearance of false concreteness. In this context Moholy himself wrote that he wished to accustom the public to 'surprises and the absence of logic'. He states: 'The frequent and unexpected appearance of the lion's head is to cause uneasiness and oppression (again and again and again). The theatre audience is cheerful — and still the head comes! etc.'

In his filmscript Moholy used the medium of photography in several ways in order to break down the automatic aspect of perception so typical of modern life:

1. In the selective isolation ('elementarization') of single motifs. This creates closeness and permits sequences with a leaping rhythmical motion as well as the superimposition of surprising associations. The appearance of false logic is broken down.

2. In the attainment of unusual views and perspectives (e.g. a railway train seen from below: something one never experiences otherwise). In this way realities which escape the natural mechanics of seeing are rendered visible. 'In everyday life a human being cannot take in many of the impressions around him. Sometimes, because his senses do not function fast enough; at other times, because moments of danger etc. claim too much of his attention. Almost everyone closes his eyes on a switchback railway during the big downward plunge. The camera does not.'[17]

3. In the rendering of concrete phenomena associated with motion as phenomena of light. Cars, furiously racing, dissolve into shimmerings or they become fast gliding spots of light on the dark asphalt. On three occasions the screen is blacked out in order to make the scene that follows the more effective as pure motion of light.

These procedures form the basis for Moholy's later active interest in photography. It is important to keep in mind that they are founded on the mobile character of film. Moholy's creative procedures contain a critique of traditional ways of perception which cannot any longer cope with the bourgeois environment or which, defeated by its misleading logic, freeze the perceiver into passivity and a creative impotence. Moholy tried to overcome the contradictions between the passive, 'creature-like' vision (symbolized by animals) and the dynamic automatism of the metropolitan tempo. He sought to give guidance for an 'active' perception of the alienated environment. It is clear that photography was for him little more than an intermediate stage between the static quality of easel painting and film, representing motion.

It is important for the reader to keep Moholy's filmscript in mind. It reveals the fundamental grounds of Moholy's own understanding of his educational commitment, grounds which often seem fated to disappear under the Constructivist rationality of his paintings, but which are really always evident in his photographs: in their motifs and content a whole series of later photographs contain references back to this filmscript.

To sum up Moholy's outline for *Dynamic of the Metropolis*: the postulate of a biological (animal) embodiment of human beings in their environment becomes dangerous at the moment when the environment escapes from intellectual control; human beings immediately become animal victims of alien forces. In the last analysis Moholy aims at a more conscious and more controlled perception by the individual of himself in his environment, and at a productive dialectic between his 'natural' and his spiritual and intellectual needs and capacities.

MANIPULATION OF LIGHT AND THE 'NEW VISION':
the photographic aspects in Moholy's art and theory

Moholy conceived his theoretical works in the context of a lively exchange of ideas with artists and writers on art with various avant-garde tendencies; he produced them, until 1929, in close collaboration with Lucia Moholy, as regards both their content and form. Lucia Moholy has thrown much light on the nature of their symbiotic oneness in work in which her scientific and systematic gifts complemented László Moholy-Nagy's bold imagination and passionate urge to realize his ideas.[18] The atmosphere in which the early writings came into being is described by Sophie Lissitzky-Küppers in her book on El Lissitzky, when she talks about his stay in Berlin in 1922. 'After work he met with his friends, either in the "Romanisches Café" or in the studio of László Moholy-Nagy, whose wife Lucia was a clever woman who took a great interest in her husband's theoretical work and helped him a great deal. Raoul Hausmann, Hannah Höch, Hans Richter and Werner Gräff (who was at that time a young motor mechanic) used to congregate in the studio.'[19]

In this constellation Moholy-Nagy's role appears to have been that of a producer of syntheses. His theories contain numerous unrelated, sometimes also eclectic elements. However, the urge to realize his ideas, as already stressed by Lucia Moholy, emerges as specifically his own. Long passages in his texts are full of proposals, partly imaginative, partly thoroughly practical, on how the ideological and practical discussions of those days might be translated into actuality. At times those writings look like belated rationalizations of practical experiments. Historical, philosophical, art-theoretical and scientific knowledge is used without hesitation to support practical solutions. This ambiguous relationship between theory and practice makes one think of Moholy's writings as being less a 'theory of art' and more of an artist's theory which bestows on his own work a systematic order and a perspective into the future. Each aspect supplements the other. All Moholy's artistic works are a series of experimental 'applications' in an overall context of ideological premises and basic propositions; they test the translation of these premises and propositions into visual techniques, and finally result in utopian projections of an art which, on the basis of experimental experience, was to undertake important projects for the future. Moholy's practice of art can be defined as a laboratory for a better tomorrow: 'as in a fever, mind and eye conquer the new dimensions of vision which today are already made available by photo and film, plan and reality. Details can wait for tomorrow. Today the mind exercizes a new vision.'[20]

To put it in a somewhat exaggerated manner, one might say that Moholy's practical as well as his theoretical work are complementary aspects of a third: their productive aspect. Artistic creatively no longer aims to produce a representation but takes on the role of being an 'instrument' with which to train and condition the new vision: it is a guide to a vital experience of the world. In Moholy's theory photography plays a decisive part and in his article called 'Production – Reproduction' of July 1922 he refers for the first time to a productive application of photography (cf. Appendix, p. 46).

The biological concept of an aesthetic 'use value' which is developed in this article is not very original. However it is interesting to note that Moholy, in an almost spectacular manner, wanted to make the 'productive' a field that until then had been regarded as a mere means of mechanical reproduction, viz. the automatism of the technical apparatus. In this appears, by way of example, the *leitmotif* of Moholy's artistic life: his wish to dissolve the automated and thereby menacing 'alien' character of the technological process of production and to open it up to individual emotional 'use'. If one continues with the 'biological' metaphor preferred by Moholy, one might say: a hitherto 'unpalatable' technology is being fermented by the understanding of the artist's ability to dissect its various elements and thus place them at the disposal of the senses. Alongside the 'symbiosis of man with nature', the instrument of which is technology, there now enters as a new dimension the 'symbiosis of man with technology'. This seemed to be necessary at a time when perception that had orientated itself hitherto by looking at 'primary nature' had begun to fail when faced with the very rapid changes occurring in the commercial and industrial environment.[21] Moholy tried to accustom the traditional natural manner of perception to a new *productive* mastery of *secondary* nature, i.e. that of a technological and urban environment. He wanted therefore to seize upon its functioning and manifestations in an *elemental* way in order to gain from it *material* for a reconstruction of perception. Moholy used photography for that purpose almost regularly and even though he was a painter, nearly all his theoretical statements on art turn, at decisive points, to categories the validity of which he tried to prove via the example of photography.

Moholy's systematic work in photography began in 1922 with his photograms. Photographs, taken with a camera, only appeared somewhat later and disappeared again almost completely from his creative work from the mid-1930s onwards. On the other hand, he continued to work on photograms throughout his working life as an artist and teacher, right up to his last years in the U.S.A.

Accordingly, Moholy's most important theoretical statements give to photograms an importance quite different from that which he accorded to camera photography. His earliest statements dating from the years 1922–25, culminating in his book *Painting, Photography, Film*, are almost exclusively concerned with the abstract optical problems posed by photograms, whilst his practical textbook on art *From Material to Architecture* (which appeared first under the title 'Through Art to Life')[22] harks back at all crucial points to camera photography. We must keep this in mind in my discussion of the photographic aspects in Moholy's art theory.

On the origins and technique of the photograms of Moholy-Nagy

The question of the 'invention' or 'discovery' of photography without a camera has been the subject of considerable dispute since the 1920s.[23] The claims to have 'discovered' this new art genre are interesting not just because of the private jealousies of individual artists but, above all, because of the special historical position of the avant-garde: the *photogram* offered an almost unique opportunity to link progress in the arts with progress in the technical means of production, and thus the resulting pictures were a valuable means for the legitimation of the position of art in the modern world. Moreover the very idea of an 'invention' was proof that artists, too, were capable of 'productive' achievements — something especially important in the volatile climate of a period of technological novelties and discoveries, in which the prestige of an Edison still stood high in popular esteem and in which Albert Einstein had become almost a living monument to the belief that the intellectual progress of humanity depended on the innovatory attainments of great individuals. The creation of photograms in laboratories also helped to lend to the procedure something of the nimbus of pioneering research. As proof of its share in Expressionist magic it is sufficient to point to such films as *The Cabinet of Dr Caligari* and *Dr Mabuse*.

At any rate the combination of art and science appeared to be an important proof of the artistic urge for 'truth'. Scholars like Wilhelm Ostwald had already worked intensively on their insight into art, indeed they looked upon art as a way to the understanding of nature. For instance, as early as 1901 Ostwald had made numerous suggestions for transparencies and *mirror images*, for paintings on *transparent sheets of glass*, *treated gelatine* or *celluloid* — suggestions that may remind us quite definitely of Moholy's later endeavours.[24] There are indeed many references to popular scientific theories in Moholy's own writings, e.g. his reference to *Bios* by Raoul Francé.[25]

In 1916 the *Photographische Korrespondenz* published an essay by Dr Bela Alexander entitled 'Räumliche Darstellung durch X-Strahlen' (spatial representation by X-rays). The author had superimposed rolls of wire netting on X-ray plates and had exposed them, obtaining in this way 'delicate and graceful moiré patterns'. He praised as 'interesting, beautiful and enjoyable' the visual results achieved in what he called — using the name of the discoverer of X-rays — 'Röntgenograms'. In 1920 Professor Paul Lindner's 'Photographie ohne Kamera' (photography without a camera) was published. Lindner photographed specially prepared substances, taken from the realm of the natural sciences, by the direct projection of parallel light rays on to sensitized paper. The results, which he called 'shadow-picture photograms' ('Schattenbildphotogramme') drove him to the brink of a kind of shadow-picture mania: 'No painter or graphic artist could ever convey the form of a leaf amid the foliage as clearly as do present-day arc lamps which, from fairly high up, project their light through the foliage of the trees of our big cities on to the pavement. How often have I not heard from people, both young and old, how beautiful are the shadows under the lime trees . . . The natural surroundings of our everyday existence are exceedingly rich in beautiful forms; we only need to be educated to discover beauty in the most insignificant of them.'[26] This rather old-fashioned concept of aesthetic education through science prepared the ground for the theories of functionalist form of the 1920s.

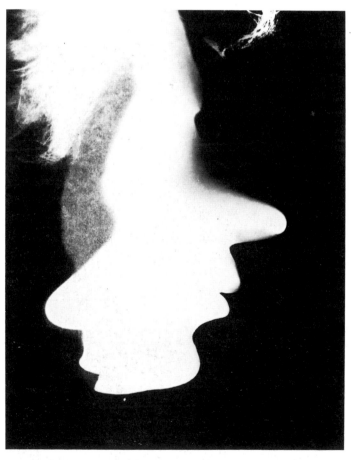

Fig. 2 László and Lucia Moholy-Nagy, *Double portrait*, a photogram dating from about 1923; a small monument to their photographic collaboration.

This term photogram is, of course, also not Moholy's invention, though it has often been claimed as such. In the technical jargon of those days it was preferred for scientific pictures, which — as was also true of microphotos, spectrograms, etc. — could be obtained by means of direct projection. One encyclopaedia of inventions, published in 1900, calls Marey's well-known chronophotographic sequence of a running man with white braids a 'photogram'.[27] Albert Einstein wrote in a letter in 1920: ' . . . Grebe's photograms are soon to appear in the *Zeitschrift für Physik.* They are really convincing, i.e. they refute current findings about the non-existence of the red-shift effect . . .'.[28] The term photogram was also introduced to designate scientifically authentic pictures; Moholy operated in just that field when he tried systematically to render 'light' visible.

As regards the question of priority in the production of artistic photograms, it has to be said that ornamental contact prints of flat objects, of feathers, silk tape, cut glass, interference patterns, flowers, and even of frost patterns had been produced since the earliest days of photography, and to some extent even before the invention of any methods of fixing permanent images. But only the development of abstract art could direct the eye away from the ornamental to the 'elemental' qualities of such forms; and it was a short step for a Dadaist — Christian Schad — to put, in 1918, a Dadaist collage (made of fabric, paper and feathers) on photographic printing paper and make prints from it.[29] The effect of Schad's pictures is rather insignificant; their special 'joke' lies in the dematerialization of the structure of materials into a state of disembodiment. They thus became a kind of parody of the genuineness of photographic images.

An essential step forward was taken by Man Ray who, starting in 1921, placed mostly three-dimensional objects on photographic paper and, by fixing the shadows they cast, obtained pictures that suggest a marked spatial quality, reminding one at times of X-ray pictures. The objects that appear are aesthetically 'sublimated' as are the 'ready-mades' of Marcel Duchamp. Man Ray, who called his pictures 'Rayographs' (also referred to as Rayograms), published a dozen of them in 1921 under the title *Champs Délicieux*, the idea for which was suggested to him by the title of André Breton's first surrealistic novel *Les Champs Magnétiques* (1919); here Breton had included a demonstration of automatic writing. Later on, Man Ray explained his invention in a typically

Fig. 3 Kurt Schwitters, *Baja*, collage, 1919.

with photograms. True, a closer collaboration between Moholy and the Berlin Dadaists after the international Dada Fair in 1920 should have made this possible; also the journeys to Paris of Huelsenbeck and Hausmann, and the publication of one of Christian Schad's photograms by Tristan Tzara in the periodical *Dadaphone* (in the March number of 1920), the frontispiece spiral of which by Picabia re-emerges in Moholy's nickel sculpture of 1921. Conceivably Huelsenbeck had referred to Rayograms as early as 1921 — in a scene of *Dr. Billig am Ende.* In the midst of the Futurist chaos of a metropolis, Margot's room in a seedy hotel opens up like a magic cell: 'a small room . . . containing human figures that are shifted around on silver bromide plates like toys . . .'[31] — the magical character of the 'Champs Délicieux' seems almost to have been captured here.

Certainly, the very first photograms of Moholy do not show the influence of Man Ray, but remind one far more of Schwitters; and Moholy does indeed mention him in connection with his own work on photograms. Just like Schwitters, Moholy in his first

Fig. 4 One of Moholy's earliest photograms, 1922.

surrealist way as being the result of an automatic 'act'. 'One sheet of photo paper got into the developing tray — a sheet unexposed that had been mixed with those already exposed under the negative . . . and as I waited in vain a couple of minutes for an image to appear, regretting the waste of paper, I mechanically placed a small glass funnel, the graduate and the thermometer in the tray on the wetted paper, turned on the light, and before my eyes an image began to form, not quite a simple silhouette of the objects as in a straight photograph, but distorted and refracted by the glass more or less in contact with the paper.'[30]

This could not have happened to Moholy-Nagy, for he was a layman in regard to photography and only became acquainted with its technique through his wife Lucia; even so, he never actually worked in the laboratory. According to his own and Lucia Moholy's statements, they had no knowledge of the work of either Schad or Man Ray when they started working

15

photograms 'de-materializes' strips of fabric and paper into transparent shades of brightness applied in a Constructivist pattern of angles. The black ground and the spatial effect of his later photograms are as yet absent.

However, Moholy did not remain for long at this early stage. Very quickly the perfectly flat character and the presence of strips running off at the edges disappear and Moholy's typical photogram makes its appearance: the non-objective spatial form, light on a black ground. Here one can find much more similarity with Man Ray, and as a matter of fact Moholy said himself that he got to know Man Ray's work in the autumn of 1922.[32] It is only now that he aims at achieving in photograms the de-materialized 'purity' of light transitions which create a vertical shading of mass and the sense of floating space. What matters for Moholy is the creation of an abstract spatial impression by means of objectless light forms. Unlike Man Ray with his magical objects appearing out of nothingness, Moholy extracts from the black field a

space, at first undefined but nevertheless real, which is gradually activated through forms of light. The forms are not individually 'put down' but owe their effect rather to a 'stepping into the light' of spatial structures that were already contained in the darkness. One might say that an 'unawakened space' now 'realizes itself' under the rays of light that fall upon it.

One recognizes that the objects whose shadows were to create the light forms of the photogram are only in minimal contact with the paper so that the shadows can be created to maximum effect. In most cases the spatial building-up occurs through light coming from different directions, causing an interplay of shadows.

At times Moholy used moving light sources so that the shadows passed continuously over the paper. In certain cases the whole production process became

Figs. 5, 6 L. Moholy-Nagy, positive and negative photographic prints, 1930.

 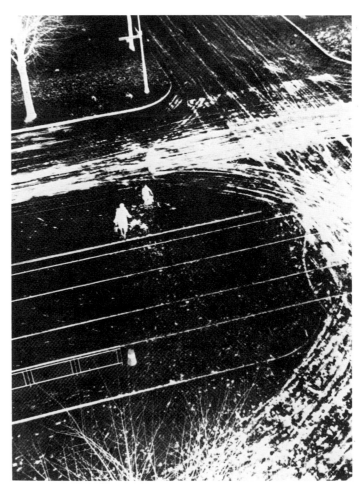

involved with time in the sense that several stages of lighting were involved (cf. note to pl. 141). This is where the strongest difference exists between Moholy and Man Ray, who worked almost exclusively with one light source and did not attempt spatial superimpositions of this sort. Moholy wrote in 1928: 'A small quantity of white is capable of keeping in balance by its activity large areas of the deepest black, and it is less a question of form than one of the quantity, direction and the positional relationships of particular manifestations of light.' He continues: 'The light-sensitive layer — plate or paper — is a tabula rasa, a blank page on which one may make notes with light just as the painter working on his canvas uses, in a sovereign manner, his tools, brush and pigment.' To be sure, there arises here the inborn paradox in the production of photograms that where the light falls there results the deepest black — that spatial nothingness — and only where the overlaid material absorbs the light will the light form become visible. Thus the light cannot be made visible directly through photography except in a reverse development, and this Moholy never applied. One cannot say with certainty whether he was ever aware of this dilemma. Once only — in 1923 — he mentions the possibility of photographing light forms, i.e. abstract projections displayed on a projection screen — a clear pointer to the reflectory light displays[34] that had been organized at the Bauhaus by Hirschfeld-Mack even before Moholy arrived there. But Moholy himself never tried to use this one possible method of using light itself as the material for a composition. At times, it is true, he had photograms copied from negative to positive, a task that could be undertaken only by an experienced photographer like Lucia Moholy (cf. pls. 133, 134), but such attempts remained rare. Evidently the results did not exercize for Moholy the same fascination as the pictures with a black ground. On the contrary, he caused even 'positive' photographs made with the camera to be converted into negative prints in order to gain an effect of bright light forms on a black ground, a result that was closer to that of a photogram.

This black ground was anticipated in the woodcuts which Moholy did simultaneously with the development of photograms and probably illustrates the closest point of connection between photography and traditional art forms in general and Moholy's ideal of light in particular. Moreover, Rodchenko's linocuts of 1918 represent a Futurist manifestation of this principle. Moholy's woodcuts are based on them:

Fig. 7   A. Rodchenko, linocut, 1918.

where the wood is actually cut away 'artistically' there appears in the woodcut the light area, the 'energy'. When Moholy says that in photography it is the *light* which *made notes* — which, so-to-speak, did the artistic work of writing — one will have to think rather of an etching in the manner of Rembrandt: where the etching tool does the most work there results the deepest black; light areas are not materially worked over. If one thinks of light replacing the artist's hand, the result is that where the light rays bombard the silver bromide most intensively, most of the silver metal is set free. Thus light creates darkness.

This logical conundrum is only resolved if one locates the 'realization' of the photogram not in the process of production but in that of looking at the

17

Fig. 8 L. Moholy-Nagy, woodcut, 1924.

'Photography is Manipulation of Light' – the significance of photograms

'Productive' manipulation

The theoretical approach adopted by Moholy to introduce his work in the field of the photogram consisted of making something 'productive' out of a technical-mechanical procedure (cf. pp. 12f.). He divided photographic procedure into separate functions, the essential one being the photo-chemical blackening of the light-sensitive surface; he now reversed the sequence of the process of production. In this way, it is not the distribution of light and shadow of a photographic negative, already frozen into a picture, which is thrown on the paper; it is rather a matter of the formation of light and shadow, originally produced solely by the lighting process, by placing objects and light-absorbing materials under fluid light rays. This results in a differentiated blackening of the paper. To follow what is going on before and during the procedure and to foresee the result is inevitably imprecise. The 'picture' appears only at the very end as the result of the various devices employed.

In 1921 Herwarth Walden wrote in his essay 'Technik und Kunst' (Technics and Art):[38] 'Every artistic creation has many and many-faceted meanings. Every technical creation has one and only one meaning.' The achievement of the photograms was to give technical creations 'many-faceted meanings' and, what is more, in the manner formulated by Herwarth Walden in the self-same essay: 'Art creates the cause of an effect such as power and movement, technics creates the effect of a cause.' By transposing the sequence of normal photographic procedure from the negative to the positive process, Moholy created the cause, namely the shadow produced by light,[39] and by means of the photo-chemical process he brought about many-faceted effects. Thus 'technics' became 'art' — to use the terminology of Expressionist theory. Moholy's modernism is quite general; it is evident not merely in his use in montages of materials produced by technical processes, such as Plexiglass, nickel etc., but, above all, in his tendency to have the work of creating forms done automatically. He 'controlled' processes at decisive stages only, and waited for a favourable conjunction without any intervention on his part. In doing this, he moved away from Constructivism in the manner of Tatlin and Lissitzky, in which the *tectonic*, the building up, the montage, is the essential aspect of their productive

work. Moholy himself had always fought against the idea of looking at photograms as if they were pictures, against subjective associations,[35] against the idea of 'a world of paintings' in the sense of Kandinsky, whose works he described as paintings of an 'undersea world'.[36] Hence Moholy also characterizes the qualities of photography in a surprisingly sensual way: 'We have gained a new feeling for the quality of chiaroscuro, luminous white, transitions from black to grey imbued with fluid light, the precise magic of the finest texture.' He describes as the 'correct treatment of photographic material' composition 'in the most delicate tones of grey and brown, with the enamel bloom of the glossy photographic paper'.[37]

18

work, and approached again the grand 'automatism' of Cézanne, who had said· 'The modelling results from a more exact relationship of tones. When these are put harmoniously next to each other, the picture models itself quite independently — one should say not so much "models" but rather "modulates".'[40] It was Moholy's artistic endeavour to imbue the disciplined organization of technical procedures with artistically 'productive' manipulation and thereby to eliminate its alien character. This is also the tendency of the de-materialized effects of the photograms and serves to explain Moholy's own hint that he had arrived at the discovery of the technique of photograms directly by way of the *MERZ* pictures of Schwitters.[41] Sibyl Moholy-Nagy makes a similar statement by quoting a saying of Schwitters dating from 1923. Materials 'receive their evaluation through the creative process. That is why I use discarded cogwheels, tissue paper, can tops, glass splinters, labels and tickets. By being balanced against each other, these materials lose their characteristics — their personality poison. They are de-materialized . . .'[42] However, in his montages Schwitters did not stop at such balancing of discarded objects, but made use of transparent materials such as gauze, veils and nets in order to produce an optical 'interpenetration' of forms. It is for this reason that Moholy's first photograms are especially reminiscent of Schwitters.

With his photograms Moholy is already coming close to the imaginative programme of Raoul Hausmann who demanded the refinement and enlargement of man's haptic sense (i.e. concerning the sense of touch) and by means of 'suitable transformers on a gigantic scale . . . the transformation of all our haptic emanations into mobile colours, noise and music of a new kind'.[43] Hausmann, who had called his friend Schwitters a great 'Umformer' (transformer),[44] must have found the basis for his idea in the gift of Schwitters for the transformation of haptic sensations with regard to materials. It was the 'tactile'[45] approach of Dadaism which sought to help the ego to have a more active entry into the world, into the 'cosmic' dimensions opened up by Russian Constructivism. Moholy had succeeded with his photograms in taking a step in the direction of transforming 'haptic' sensations into the impression of a spatial emanation in terms of Hausmann's theory. The forms of light in Moholy's photograms are at once distant and near and in the formation of shadow-casting masses they reveal a spatial — optical as well as

a plastic — haptic character. Moholy had even found a symbol for the sublimation of the haptic, of that which could be touched by hand. In his silhouette of a hand (fig. 9) the automatic process of creation is revealed: the open hand is shown as inactive, just in an imploring gesture, at the intersection of spatial lines, and without holding any tool — in contrast to the famous hand-montage by Lissitzky which shows a

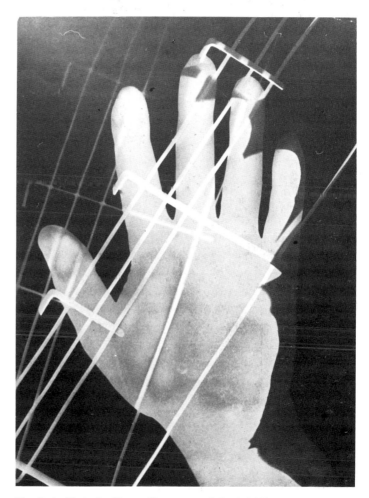

Fig. 9 L. Moholy-Nagy, Photogram (cf. pl. 140).

hand holding a pair of compasses. Moholy used this hand-photogram a second time (fig. 11), this time in a manner even more closely reminiscent of Lissitzky but at the same time decisively distanced from him: Lissitzky's montage includes a lively looking, active eye at the centre of the active hand; the pair of compasses, the hand and the eye, technical-scientific, manual and intellectual-artistic work, refer to each other. Moholy includes at the same spot in the

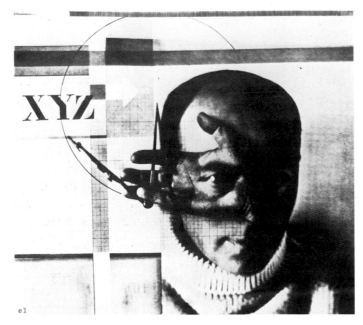

Fig. 10 El Lissitzky, *The Constructor* (self-portrait), 1924

Fig. 11 L. Moholy-Nagy, title-page for the journal *Foto-Qualität*, Dessau 1931.

passively open hand, the automatic 'photo-eye'. Human creation is still only regulated, as if in a conjuring act, by mechanical devices.

The theory of 'Light'

The mechanization of the process of production and the concentration of 'manipulation' on 'regulating' devices changed decisively the quality of artistic production and was variously reflected in Moholy's work. Most revealing is his statement : 'My desire was to go beyond the apparent into the realm of objective validity, serving the public as an anonymous agent . . . My photographic experiments, especially photograms, helped to convince me that even the complete mechanization of technics may not constitute a menace to its essential creativeness.'[46] The points he makes are connected. Moholy saw 'objective validity' in the elemental purity of the optical means of expression which were to be falsified as little as possible by the association of objects and the individuality and materiality of the craft and technique of composition. The forms of photograms without objects and texture, composed by light, could be regarded in this respect as the ideal means of pure presentation.

Moholy's aim is to be described as the 'objectivization' of the subjective-expressionist desire for self-

expression. This desire is to be realized by a systematic breakdown of the means of expression and their renewed combination using the phenomena of modern technical developments. If Moholy regarded himself as an 'anonymous agent'[47] of the public, it was his wish to prepare visual representations of the environment in such a way that they could be used by the individual observer as a means of self-expression, for the projection of his own desire to express himself in the environment.

Malevich wrote, in a letter to Moholy, of his own art having 'as its content non-objective sensations that bring me into harmony with the universe'.[48] Moholy expressed himself similarly, if a shade more 'functionalistically' : 'Thought — as functional result of cosmos-body interaction — is in its manifestations a constant emanation of human existence . . . the immanent mind seeking light — light'.[49] As light, according to Moholy, is an element of the mind, and yet simultaneously does the actual 'work' of producing art, there results the strange, almost magical, aspect of an immaterial artistic creation through spiritual emanation.

However, in his rational explanations Moholy strongly rejected such suggestions for his photograms and left the 'magical' sector to Man Ray. 'As an obvious consequence of my painting (which belongs to the field of optical manipulation) I understood photograms differently from May Ray. The elementary function of photographic procedures consists in the domination of light intensities, in the transposition of black into white, in the transitions from lightness into darkness. The optical miracle of black into white is to result from the dematerialised radiation of light without any literary secrets or secret associations, through the elimination of pigment and texture. All secondary and imitative effects, even the very memory of them, are to be excluded. Photograms have to be produced by their own primary means, signifying, in their construction, nothing but themselves . . . Only here one can speak of the slowly emerging relationship with light, that substance so difficult to grasp, of creating an organically conscious awareness of its enigma. Accordingly I have concentrated in my experiments on producing most delicate transitions from hard-white to black intensities that have an effect of their own. Sometimes, without intending it, I got pictures with almost cosmical and astronomical effects. I tried to avoid this as I see in it the disadvantage of having complexes of material associations.'[50]

It is, however, significant that intuitive remarks always tend to obscure the meaning of Moholy's rational statements: ' . . . Its essence is a never-failing certitude of feeling vis-à-vis the appearance of light – of its activity in brightness, of its passivity in the dark – its most delicate distribution of rays to the point of a perfect balance between the values of very small and very great tensions.'[51] That it was possible at all to speak of *light* in this substantially intuitive manner again appears to be only possible by way of a rationalization of *spiritual* claims such as those that were voiced by Lothar Schreyer in the Expressionist mysticism of those years: 'The aim of the work of art is the illumination of the inner light. The forces unfold their power in the artist and teach him that he himself is this power which is more than the visible man. They link him with all the luminosity of light in its manifestations. He who wishes to announce the light, has to live in the light. Darkness gives birth to the light. He who wishes to shine, must be light . . .'.[52]

The manipulation of light as the manipulation of motion

The 'meaning' contained in Moholy's constant references to light as a means of manipulation is more easily understood if one goes back (as already noted above) to what lies behind the Constructivist debate in the 1920s, and regards Moholy's earliest initiatives in the context of subjective Expressionism. Moholy's endeavours had turned on the problem of mediating between the subjectivist claims of Expressionism and the 'productive' category postulated by the Constructivists. The question whether Moholy's synthesis of Expressionist ideals with Constructivist realism signifies progress cannot be answered in general terms. Rather it can only be posed in those cases where Moholy's aesthetic categories can be related to concrete perceptions of the environment. Within the abstract ideology of light represented by the photograms this is possible in one category above all others – that of motion.

Moholy frequently spoke of 'fluid light'.[53] He even said: 'Generally speaking, the manifestations of light are fluid, and all photographic procedures achieve their highest point in film (the fluid relationship of light projection).'[54] Thus the 'motion of the photogram' with which Moholy enriched photography becomes a turning point from static to kinetic manipulation. Photography, regarded as a manipulation of light, may be regarded as the essential means for achieving the 'vision in motion' aimed at by Moholy.

In the first (German) edition of *Painting Photography Film* (1925; see Bibliography), Moholy linked the abstract concept of 'motion' to the modernistic idea of 'tempo'.[55] and he concluded his book with a list of pictures used in his filmscript *Dynamic of the Metropolis* which had attempted, by means of a hectic cutting process, to realize an optical arrangement of tempo.[56] This achievement of Moholy reminds one of Ludwig Meidner's Expressionist and Futurist *Guide to the Painting of Pictures of a Metropolis*, published as early as 1913. For Meidner, too, the showing of the tempo of a metropolis had been 'first and foremost a problem of light'. 'We do not perceive in nature a ubiquitous presence of light, we see frequently in front of us large areas, seemingly frozen, which appear to be unlit; here and there we sense heaviness, darkness, immobile matter. The light seems to flow. It splits objects. We clearly sense scraps of light, light strips,

Fig. 12 Ludwig Meidner, *I and the City*, 1913.

clusters of light. Whole complexes are swaying in light and appear to be transparent — yet in between there is again rigidity and the opacity of broad masses of matter. Between rows of high buildings we are blinded by a tumult of brightness and darkness. Walls are displaying broad surfaces of light. Amongst the crowd of heads a light rocket explodes. Light flashes brightly between vehicles. The sky invades us like a waterfall. Its plentitude of light dissolves what is below. Sharp contours sway in glaring brightness. There are fleeing hosts of rectangles in swirling rhythms. Light sets in motion everything all around. Towers, houses and lanterns seem to be suspended in the air or to swim . . .'[57]

Moholy includes the following sequences: 'Warehouses and cellars — darkness — DARKNESS — Becoming gradually lighter — Railway. Highway (with vehicles). Bridges, Viaduct. Water below. Boats in waves. Cable railway above. Shot of a train taken from a bridge: from above; from below. (The belly of a train as it passes . . .)' etc. 'Glass lift in a warehouse with a negro attendant. Oblique. Perspective distorted. Chiaroscuro. View out. Tumult. The dogs tethered at the entrance. Next to the glass lift a glass telephone box with a man telephoning. View THROUGH. Shot of the ground floor through the glass panes. TEMPO-O TEMPO-O . . .' etc. — 'The vehicles: electric trains, cars, lorries, bicycles, cabs, bus, cyclonette, motor-cycles travel in quick time from the central point outwards, then all at once they change direction; they meet at the centre. The centre opens, they ALL sink deep, deep, deep — a wireless mast. (The camera is swiftly tilted over; there is a sense of plunging downwards.) Under the tramways the sewers being extended. Light reflected in the water. TEMPO TEMPO-O-O. ARC-LAMP, sparks playing. Street smooth as mirror. Pools of light. From above and oblique with cars whisking past. Reflector of a car enlarged. — SCREEN BLACK FOR 5 SECONDS — Electric signs with luminous writing which vanishes and reappears . . . YMOHOLYMOH . . . Fireworks from the Lunapark. Speeding along WITH the scenic railway . . .'[58]

Moholy creates *dynamics* by dramatic and rhythmical leaps from one 'element' to the other. Meidner still thinks of the phenomenon of motion as a continuum in the sense of Impressionism, even though it is turbulent and its rays are fragmented. In consequence Meidner's environment, by being totally in motion, becomes alien and threatening to human consciousness whilst Moholy compels the consciousness of the perceiver to participate actively in the motion of leaping from image to image.

Both artists translate the phenomenon of motion into manifestations of light but here, too, there are similar differences in their concrete presentation. Meidner makes mobile objects appear as if driven by light or dissolved by light; its energy eats into towers and walls of houses, and causes them to sway. The tempo of the metropolis is the tempo of *traffic*; the movements of the means of transport, of human beings and of commodities obey the pressure for profit of the overriding power which Meidner presented in an almost apocalyptic vision of light.

For Moholy, on the contrary, light is not an alien, external driving force but it 'arises' out of the dark and becomes itself the very substance of motion. The manifestations of light in film, with their ever-fluid luminosity unfolding in the dark surroundings, remind one immediately of the light effects in the photograms

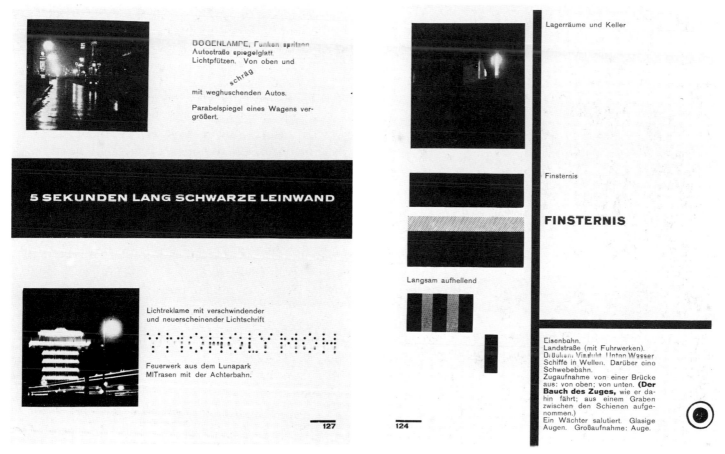

Figs. 13, 14 L. Moholy-Nagy, typophotos from the filmscript *Dynamik der Großstadt* ('Dynamic of the Metropolis'), 1921–24 — black screen and darkness.

which Moholy had discovered at that time. In these pictures light takes on the character of a *haptic* image. Significantly, Moholy speaks of his intention to create 'a relationship with light, that substance so difficult to grasp[!]' and to 'create an organically conscious awareness of its enigma'.[59] Or he writes: 'Contrary to the usual idea that photography has reached its ultimate in imitation, it must be stressed that the ability to freeze manifestations of light to the point of being grasped[!] is not shared by any other procedure.'[60] It seems to be possible to overcome alienation and to regain the penetrating and appropriating closeness of the perceiving subject to the environment when light, the bearer of optical perception, is regarded as a substance and, in the meaning of *elemental* art, the qualities of external phenomena and of subjective feeling are brought into concrete proximity to each other.

This is illustrated in the focussing of the image in the luminous writing: 'YMOHOLYMOH'. In it there appears a strangely exalted light-like projection of the artist in the blackness of the metropolitan tumult. Commenting on his filmscript, Moholy describes it as his aim 'to integrate the viewer actively in the dynamics of the city'.[61] He also tells us that institutions and film companies had refused to make use of his filmscript and goes on to note that there were only a few painters who were still experimenting on their own: 'This work is received with suspicion, and one cannot be offended on account of such suspicion, for the technique of film-production, the whole paraphernalia no longer admits of private effort...'.[62] In this situation the photograms were the basis of an art which experienced the dilemma of wanting to collaborate 'in the creative work of its own time with up-to-date means'[63] and yet was unable to

23

Fig. 15 Constantin Brancusi, *Sculpture for blind people* or *The Beginning of the World*, 1924.

make use of contemporary means of production, thus remaining dependent for the creation of its incunabula on individual and private effort instead of the collective one dreamed of by the artists.

Moholy's manipulation of light makes sense for us when it remains related to concrete reality; for instance, when it makes the attempt to create a novel and more intensive consciousness of time and motion or to awaken sensitivity to rich and differentiated values of forms and tones – i.e. to educate people to acquire an optical perception of forms in the modern environment. Only if the particular beauty of a photogram arouses human consciousness to experience aesthetic feelings is it also a means for overcoming the alienation of reality.

Four concepts: 'Time', 'Floating', 'Space', 'Modulation'

Moholy's quality as an artist stands and falls with his ability to keep to the dialectic relationships with reality into which Expressionist metaphysics had, in his own situation, been transformed. His urge to create vision in motion is closely connected with the motion of time. When, at the end of the 1920s, he produced his abstract film *Light Display, Black and White and Grey*,[64] his purpose was to create a 'light chronology' by means of the gradation of brightness alone. He himself thought that the technique of the photogram had played a clarifying part in this: 'The key to the manipulation of light is the "photogram", photography without a camera. Its numerous gradations into black-white and its fluid values of tones (later on, to be sure, also of colour values) are of fundamental significance.'[65]

Since the turn of the century the perception of time had played an important part in aesthetic theory. Bergson defended his concept of *durée*, i.e. the expansion and intensification of the sense of time as intuitively experienced by the subject, against its reification in consequence of economic ends which had made of time a rationally quantifiable and measurable value. Something similar was meant by Kandinsky when he wrote in *Point and Line to Plane* – entirely in the spirit of Malevich – about the dematerialization of the material base plane of painting: 'The elements lying firmly (materially) on a solid, more or less hard and, to the eye, tangible BP and, in contrast, to the elements "floating" without material weight in an indefinable (immaterial) space are of fundamentally different appearance and stand in antithesis to each other' – and he added the following note: 'It is clear that the transformation of the material plane and the general character of the elements combined with it are certain to have important consequences in many respects. One of the most important of these is the change in the feeling for time: space is identical with depth; also with the elements receding into depth. It is not without reason that I have called the space resulting from dematerialization "indefinable" – its depth is, after all, illusory and, therefore, not exactly measurable. Thus time cannot in these cases be expressed in figures and so it cooperates only relatively. On the other hand, the illusory depth is an actual one from a pictorial point of view and consequently a certain, even though immeasurable, time is required to follow the form elements receding into depth. Therefore: the transformation of the material BP into indefinable space offers the opportunity of increasing the span of time.'[66]

Here one has to think of Moholy, who took great care in his painting to make the material base plane of the painting disappear but, significantly, no longer by 'painterly' equivalents but by the use of objective means. 'Experiments with painting on highly polished black panels (trolite), on coloured transparent and translucent plates (galalith, matt and translucent Cellon), produce strange optical effects: it looks as though the colour were *floating* almost without material effect in a space in front of the plane to which it is in fact applied.'[67]

In this connection photograms prove to be an extremely 'rational' procedure for the production of similar effects. They too, have no *base plane*, the light floats in space, it creates relationships in depth which cannot be measured and thereby offers (as Kandinsky says) an opportunity for enlarging the sense of time.

Moholy's aim in the presentation of motion is to create a subjective experience of time. In 1922 he pronounced that 'man, heretofore merely receptive in his observation of works of art, experiences a heightening of his own faculties, and becomes himself an active partner to the forces unfolding themselves'.[68]

If we ask ourselves why Moholy preferred working with light in the manipulation of time and motion, it must be remembered that in Einstein's theory of relativity the hitherto 'absolute' categories of time and space had become 'relative' and only light remained as an immutable constant of nature. Furthermore, this idea had been adopted and popularized just then in philosophical thinking. Einstein's theory of relativity helped to make possible the notion of light being treated as a 'substance', to re-define mystical ideas of 'fluid' light in a rational form, and to enable light to be considered an actual 'material means' for manipulation (see above, pp. 21ff.).

Moholy's work with light, which he regarded as an absolute substance, is best described by the word 'modulation', used by him later on. Light as such is not visible in space unless it is reflected by objects. It discloses its character as the mobile energy of light rays only in the modulation of shadows. In this manner every object in space becomes a light modulator, by means of which light is made to exist individually and accidentally, and has its existence in time and space.

Moholy's concept of motion is not one of energy and dynamics, as is that of the Futurists, but of the modulation of existing energies in time and space.

The 'New Vision' – the role of camera photography in Moholy's work

Before 1925, when the first edition of Moholy's book *Painting, Photography, Film* appeared, he had only once made a public statement on the use of representational photography. In the catalogue for the Bauhaus exhibition of 1923 he had published an article on 'The New Typography', in which he had described how the employment of photographs in graphic design acted as an amplification of information through elements capable of quite exact expression: 'Photographs, both large and small, are today being used in the text, taking the place of concepts and expressions themselves capable of individual interpretation. The objective quality of photography releases the previously receptive person from, for example, the crutch of a personal description, and he will be driven more than was formerly the case to forming his own opinion.'[69]

The first time Moholy tried to treat representational photography in his own way was when he published his book in 1925. All his efforts were concentrated on the description of novel sensations of light and motion. The representational capacity of photography

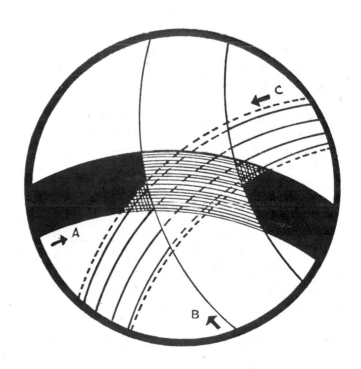

Fig. 16 L. Moholy-Nagy, schematic drawing for simultaneous projections, 1925.

25

provided hardly more than pictorial raw material for manipulation — especially in the section on 'Typophoto' and 'Simultaneous (or poly) cinema'. Though Moholy begins his book with the complex host of problems indicated by such key words as 'objective' and 'non-objective', he talks about the character of photography with a camera on one page only, albeit decisively, when he mentions its achievements, 'with the aid of the photographic camera to make visible existences which cannot be perceived or taken in by our optical instrument, the eye'.[70] The camera can perfect the eye and supplement it, e.g. by scientific close-ups and mobile shots etc.: '. . . the photographic camera reproduces the purely optical image and therefore shows the optically true distortions, deformations, foreshortenings etc.'.[71] In the revised edition of the book (1927) he added this important passage: 'Thus in the photographic camera we have the most reliable aid to a beginning of objective vision. Everyone will be compelled to see what is optically true, is explicable in its own terms, is objective, before he can arrive at any possible subjective position.'[72] However, it is of critical importance that Moholy did not attach any creative significance to this objectivity of the camera picture but saw in it merely the basic material for actual artistic production. 'We may say that we see the world with entirely different eyes. Nevertheless, the total result to date amounts to little more than a visual encyclopaedic achievement. This is not enough. We wish to *produce* systematically, since it is important for life that we create *new relationships*.'[73] After these words the book proceeds to speak of photograms, the typophoto and film. In the first edition of 1925 (the content of which Moholy said had been put together in 1924) there was not a single camera photo by him. The illustrations consisted exclusively of photograms, photomontages and the typophoto for the filmscript *Dynamic of the Metropolis*.[74]

This typophoto illustrates best how Moholy at that time regarded the potential of photography for placing isolated 'moments' in kinetic relationships with each other. Photography contained for him a new potential for conveying motion, a new possibility for passing beyond the static plate and pressing directly forward towards film. For him this was the *productive* field. Through active, synoptic manipulation the viewer was to become in his own person the 'executor' of the constellation of elements and thereby the subject that achieved a synthesis of a total

perception of reality. '*Kunst baut auf*'[75] (art builds up, constructs) was the key phrase with which Moholy characterized its *productive* aspect. Important for him were 'the capacity and the courage to build up *new* relations among the elements of expression, to raise them above the commonplace by giving them a new interpretation — sometimes through shifting their meaning'.[76] Moholy traced the *productive* value of art, in the sense of a biological and aesthetic 'use value', quite logically back to its capacity 'to seize the original, to own it personally'.[77] This capacity had been raised from a material to a 'psychological' level. 'The aim was no longer the reproduction of objects in the search for a resemblance of life . . . but the establishment of relations of volume, material, mass, shape, direction, position and light.'[78]

Moholy appears to have been particularly fascinated by the fact that photography could not merely deal with the 'elements' of static single details but that it was also able to make visible 'continuous' procedures so that they could become elements of the 'progression of time'. Thus Moholy photographed from the air a mountain formation, making visible the changes in the formation of the earth's surface, as in a time compressor.[79] In this way many surfaces can be understood as 'traces of time'. Moholy's most famous example can be seen in the wrinkled face of a 130-year-old man, about which he made this fanciful comment: 'The photograph of the old man is essentially a time-compressing view of the alteration of the epidermis: an aerial photograph of time.'.[80]

The obsession with the totality of time as an element of alien determination, which we still find in Impressionist paintings, seems to have been eliminated in such presentations. If it wanted to 'save' itself, the totally atomized subject in the time continuum of Monet's or Pissarro's crowded streets in a big city had only the possibility of extrapolating itself into aesthetic 'distance', of rising above the crowd and — as Kandinsky said — 'of contemplating the world through a window pane'.[81] From this point of view a tactile intervention in these movements was not possible. The turbulence could merely still provide 'nutriment to the ''flâneur'', slowly and luxuriously sauntering through town or withdrawing to the heights'[82] by mounting a tower (at that time the Eiffel Tower was attracting much attention). For all others the motion in time of metropolitan traffic had been corrupted by the alienated power of economic pressures: 'time is money'. Those who practised

Fig. 17 Street junction in New York.

Naturalism, at the end of the nineteenth century, were occasionally in despair because of this tight 'mechanization' of mobility, and they produced fatalistic pictures of the primordial causality of all things and the de-personalization of human beings in these conditions.[83]

Only Cubism (actually only Picasso), Dadaism and Constructivism found — artistically — the dialectical 'gaps' in this mechanization. The causal continuum was opened up towards dialectics.[84] General relationships and the relationship to distance were enlarged to become fields of tension in which human consciousness could function 'creatively'. Here begins the attempt at a tactile perception in relation to the environment which had to achieve new elemental forms of perception.

Moholy's attitude was resolute. He drew on photography as the new standard language for the aesthetic intervention of the technical environment. 'It is sufficiently unprecedented that such a "mechanical" thing as photography, and one regarded so contemptuously in an artistic and creative sense, should have acquired the power it has, and become one of the primary objective visual forms in barely a century of evolution . . . Through photography, too, we can participate in new experiences of space, and in even greater measure through the film. With their help, and that of the new school of architects, we have attained an enlargement and sublimation of our appreciation of space . . . Thanks to the photographer,

humanity has acquired the power of perceiving its surroundings, and its very existence, with new eyes. But all these are isolated characteristics, separate achievements, not altogether dissimilar to those of painting. In photography we must learn to seek, not the "picture", not the aesthetic of tradition, but the ideal instrument of expression, the self-sufficient vehicle for education.'[85]

'Comprehending Vision' — from the haptic to the optical

With Moholy the 'instrumentalist' understanding of photography becomes a question of 'tactics', of the 'use value' inasmuch as 'tactics' demands the planned employment of given means for the achievement of definite aims. An autonomous environment with dynamics of its own can no more be used with such intent and is closed to intervention by tactics. Walter Benjamin used the concept of the 'tactile' in contrast to the 'optical' when he wished to characterize the two ways of considering architecture, by 'use' and by 'perception'.[86] This contrast is reminiscent of the opposites 'tactile-haptic' in Alois Riegl's 'artistic intention' (*Kunstwollen*). According to this, the 'haptic'[87] would have been regarded as inherent in the 'tactile', as is anyhow suggested by the category of 'use'. If we view Moholy from this standpoint, his intention of turning the purely 'optical' into the 'tactile' through the inclusion of 'haptic' qualities becomes surprisingly clear. His second main theoretical work, *Von Material zu Architektur* (1929; English version, *The New Vision: From Material to Architecture*), in which he gave his practical directions for the application of Bauhaus art theory, is to be understood in this sense.

The declared aim of this art theory was 'man as a whole. Man — when faced with the material and spiritual problems of life — can, if he works from his biological centre, take his position with instructive success. Then he is in no danger of intimidation by industry, the haste of an often misunderstood "machine culture", or by past philosophies about his creative ways.'[88] The people at the Bauhaus had to 'learn to master not only themselves, but also the living and working conditions of the environment . . . the educational program of the Bauhaus, or more exactly, its working program, rests upon this.'[89]

The endeavour to 'master' the environment — a 'tactical' concept — culminates on the last pages of the book in an almost hymnal invocation of a new architecture of the future as consciousness of space: 'Openings and boundaries, perforations and moving surfaces, carry the periphery to the centre, and push the centre outward. A constant fluctuation, sideways and upwards, radiating, all-sided, announces that man has taken possession, so far as his human capacities and conceptions allow, of imponderable, invisible and yet omnipresent space.'[90]

At this point Moholy, the artist, has to be distinguished from Benjamin, the philosopher — the active manner from the contemplative one. Benjamin had considered that there were only two possible ways of appreciating a work of art, and these are both relatively passive: on the one hand there is 'optical' concentration and contemplative 'absorption' in looking at a work of art; on the other hand there is the casual approach of an otherwise preoccupied crowd getting accustomed to the (architectural) work of art. But these ways were not sufficient for Moholy. Instead of getting accustomed, he demanded an active way of taking possession and put next to contemplative 'absorption' the 'activity' of the viewer which was to be stimulated by kinetic art.[91] Benjamin's lament about the loss of the artistic 'aura' is no longer relevant to Moholy's instrumental concept of art, least of all to his conviction that in photography is to be found the proper instrument for education and expression.[92] Moholy used it in this sense in his book *Von Material zu Architektur.*

We shall not occupy ourselves further with Moholy's not very consistently defined or applied system of the three haptic categories of structure, texture and surface treatment. However, in this context we must single out the concept of *surface treatment* (*Faktur*) as it is central to Moholy's exposition and becomes a particular problem in photography. Moholy says: 'Surface aspect (or surface treatment) means the sensorily perceptible result (the effect) of a working process as shown by any given treatment of materials. Such a change in the material surface through external factors may be brought about in different ways; . . . Surface aspects may be due to elemental causes, such as the influence of nature, or to mechanical causes, such as machine treatment.'[93] Moholy's equation of the natural and the *human* treatment of materials is decisive from the point of view of both method and ideology. In this way, without hesitation he 'naturalized' the entire category of material work and divested it of all social attachment. The individually felt category of a

working process is transferred from subjective experience to phenomena far removed from the subject. Thus they are brought close to the 'tactile' sensation. However, in the course of his book, Moholy states that the *essential* element of manipulation is 'the importance of volume, which surpasses the material effects of the treatment of surfaces [*Faktur*] to the point of the complete sublimation (abstraction) of relationships'.[94] At this juncture the most important role in his presentation is played by photographic examples.

For instance, only the frozen snapshot makes the transformation of *mass* into volume, i.e. of convex into concave space, aimed at by Moholy, a startling experience for the eye; and Moholy illustrated many Cubist sculptures which demonstrate that effect.[95] Long shots (e.g. of a merry-go-round in motion) allow the 'virtual volume' of moving objects to become visible.[96] 'Sculpture is the path to the freeing of a material form from its weight: from mass to motion.'[97] Photography could now easily transform into an actual perception of nature what before had been regarded as a mere 'optical illusion' in the psychology of perception. Similarly, only the rigid black-and-white projection on to a plane of one-eyed shots, with their extremely limited spatial information, could give an impulse to the application of concepts like structure, texture and surface treatment, irrespective of the definition of objects, their material and aggregate state (fluid, solid, loose, rigid): thus the standard measure was no longer external reality but the photographic picture that systematically unified all objects as to their scale and substance. In 1901 Alois Riegl tried to define the *Kunstwollen* (artistic intention) of a period by way of its perception and treatment of space, making this the supreme criterion of aesthetics.[98]

Moholy's book *From Material to Architecture* was still based on this idea; it culminated in the treatment of *space.* In it Moholy declared point blank: 'Space is a reality, and once it has been comprehended in its essence, it can be grasped according to its own laws . . . spatial creation is the creation of relationships of the position of bodies (volumes).'[99] Thus space existed for Moholy as an absolute *substance* but could only be comprehended and manipulated in the accidental form of specific relationships. This idea continues throughout Moholy's entire theory of manipulation, with photography and painting complementing each other.

Regarding the *active* manipulation of space, Moholy wrote: 'Space is known first of all by the sense of vision. This experience of the visible relations of bodies may be checked by movement — by the alteration of one's position — and by means of touch. From the point of view of the subject, space can be experienced most directly by movement, on a higher level, in the dance. The dance is an elemental means for realization of space-creative impulses. It can articulate space, order it.'[100] The subject in motion experiences space, and simultaneously actively manipulates it.

In a general sense Moholy's artistic production is the attempt to create for the viewer a 'reciprocal' effect between the active manipulation of space and the work of art.

Constructivist and Chaplin perspectives
In 1922, together with Alfred Kemény (who shortly before had visited the Constructivists in the Soviet Union), Moholy wrote the manifesto 'The Dynamic-Constructive System of Forces'. There they state *inter alia*: 'Constructivism means the activation of space by means of a dynamic-constructive system of forces, that is the constructing within one another of forces actually at tension in physical space . . . We must therefore put in the place of the static principle of classical art the dynamic principle of universal life . . . Carrying further the unit of construction, a dynamic-constructive system of force is attained, whereby man, heretofore merely receptive in his observation of works of art, experiences a heightening of his own faculties, and becomes himself an active partner with the forces unfolding themselves. The first projects . . . can be only experimental . . . Next comes the utilization of the experimental results for the creation of freely moving (free from mechanical and technical movement) works of art.'[101]

In El Lissitzky's article which he called 'Proun' (written in 1920 and published in 1922) we find the following statements: ' . . . the artist, having been an imitator, is becoming the builder of a new world of objects . . . Proun is a creative manipulation (domination of space) by means of the economic construction of revalued material . . . One builds as in three-dimensional space and therefore we must here, too, in the first place balance the tensions of the particular positions. We have set Proun into motion and thus we gain a plurality of projection axes; we stand between them and push them apart . . .'.[102]

Fig. 18 *On the steel-and-concrete girder*, about 1928.

Fig. 19 *Decorating work*, 1925 (as illustrated in Roh; cf. note to pl. 7).

29

Fig. 20 Dziga Vertov, *The Man with the Camera*.

This *activating* manner of seeing is transferred to the camera by Lissitzky's closest co-fighters, by Rodchenko in photography and by Dziga Vertov in film. These artists made of the photo or film camera an eye with a long perspective which dissects the elements of its objects from above and below, which circles around them and steps between them.[103] However, Moholy's aim was not the 'domination of space by means of construction' (Lissitzky) but by means of mobile *perception.* If Lissitzky was a constructor, Moholy was a painter. Only on this assumption could it occur to him to transfer the Constructivist principle of manipulation to the reduced optical form of a photographic picture and thereby to neglect completely the 'activating' arrangements of the Russians.

Socialist photography as influenced by Rodchenko tried to depict workers from their own point of view and to obtain their active involvement. Moholy, however, always remained on the side of the 'consumer' or user who looked critically at the manifestations of modern production — at its 'technique' as much as at its possible utilization in a metropolis and its capacity to create new aesthetic experiences.

Moholy, too, climbed radio towers, photographed the balconies of the Bauhaus obliquely from below, and took pictures of building sites and concrete pipes. However, he did not 'build up' an object, 'resulting' from motion; rather he built up a subject that 'resulted' from suggested perspectives.[104]

Moholy changed Constructivism into the construction of the living 'self' of the viewer by means of suggesting the virtual motion of the subject in space. This points away from the Russians in the direction of Dadaism. Moholy's position lay between Constructivism and Dadaism. At that time, amidst bourgeois rigidity, Charlie Chaplin was the incarnation of 'mobility'. The International Dada Company in Berlin had sent Charlie Chaplin, 'the greatest artist in the world, and good Dadaist', hearty greetings and assurances of sympathy.[105] Moholy, too, created his Chaplin image, which only too clearly demonstrates — if not actually exaggerates — the connection between perspective and mobile existence that is so important for our presentation.

Moholy's photomontage (fig. 21) has several titles, among them *City Lights* and *Da stehst du machtlos vis à vis* ('There you stand powerless face to face'): the smallish Chaplin figure gets from below an extremely distorted view of two fat women in bathing

Fig. 21 L. Moholy-Nagy, photomontage *City Lights*, 1936.

costumes; he is forced into this perspective and his only reaction is that he stretches his head just a little as if looking over a fence. The erotic theme contributes to the intended impression; he alone is active. Thus, despite his fragility, he can compete with the two massive and passive women. Once the perspective is 'corrected' so that we see the women in front and Charlie behind, the women become ridiculously small and Charlie almost looks athletic – or at any rate like the hero of the situation, as is always the point of his films, i.e. the one who appears at first the weakest, the one who is most easily pushed around, becomes in the end the 'victor' because of the trick of the reversal of the relations of strength and because he knows best how to use the situation (he has the bottom 'view'). He himself is never 'good' or 'the hero'; it is the circumstances that give him the upper hand.

Every photographic picture has a central perspective because of the very shape and construction of the camera. In judging 'new views' in photography one has to be conscious of this. Whether photographs are taken vertically, looking down from scaffolding, or up the façades of houses, a virtual viewpoint necessarily results from the perspective as presented.

Elementarization: photography and abstract art
Moholy did not stop at the simple classification of the elements of material manifestations in terms of structure, texture and surface treatment and their transformation into photographic light phenomena. Intending to verify in reality the achievements of modern art, he also tried to subject creativity to the basic forms of abstract art. This becomes quite clear in his predilection for the basic elements of Suprematism: circle, cross and square.

An example of this treatment occurs in Moholy's highly intentional combination of crossed knives with the rounded forms of crockery (fig. 23). In order to separate the elements of the concrete world in such a 'Suprematist' way, one needs well-chosen, out-of-the-ordinary viewpoints, from which true perception of objects is obscured through unusual foreshortenings and overlapping in favour of abstract figures.

The influence of Constructivism becomes even clearer when (as in Lissitzky) the Suprematist elements approximate to material and spatial bodies whose relationship is one of spatial tension with each other. However, here the decisive difference between Moholy's photography and painting becomes evident: painting – especially Constructivist painting –

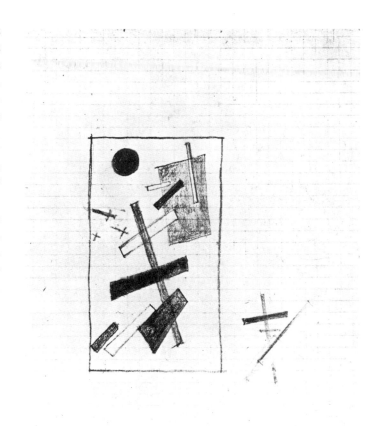

Fig. 22 K. Malevich, Suprematist drawing, 1915/16.

builds up the picture from single elements. The camera, on the contrary, takes, more or less arbitrarily, a single extract from the continuum of perception. If the photographer wants to realize any precise intentions, he has to be 'mobile'. Moholy certainly 'discovered' with naïve cleverness properties in the camera which allowed him to take approximately Constructivist pictures. However, it was not possible in this manner to make the specific reality of the objective world completely subject to the 'creative intention'. The dialectic between the subject and the continuum of things remains and Moholy began gradually exploiting it positively, in his own way. Here then, beyond all 'artistic intention' and perhaps at first unconsciously, his specifically 'photographic' achievement becomes manifest.

First of all, there appear in the picture – more or less 'automatically' – not just the constellation of objects but, as an additional spatial system, the projection of

31

Fig. 23 L. Moholy-Nagy, *Lucia Moholy at the breakfast table*, about 1926 (cf. pl. 4).

oblique lines and co-ordinates of the pictures are at sharp angles to the picture margins and therefore create a strong contrast to the right angles of the frame. Here Moholy came close to the intention of his friend Theo van Doesburg who, like himself, was associated with Dadaism and had moved away more and more from the pre-established harmony of Mondrian (with whom he had originally founded De Stijl, in which movement both artists had been representative figures).

In 1926, in an article called 'Painting: From Composition to Counter-Composition', van Doesburg had defined his new standpoint thus: 'We execute our physical movements in the horizontal-vertical direction. Through the continual repetition of these natural

Fig. 24 L. Moholy-Nagy, *Hotel terrace on Belle-Ile-en-Mer*, 1925 (cf. pl. 20).

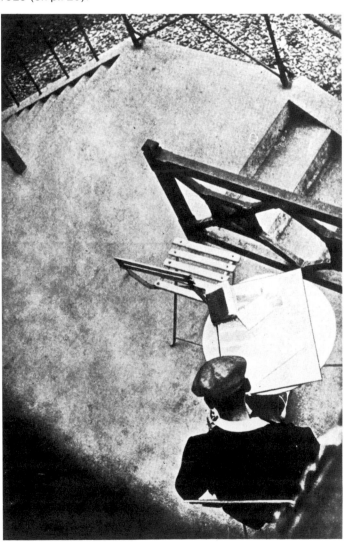

their light and their shadows (cf. pls. 2, 3, 4). In this way two spatial systems interpenetrate and are superimposed on each other; of these only the objective system has a perspective relationship to the viewer whilst the projection of shadows appears to be alien, as if brought in from outside. Thus the picture suddenly gains a spatial life of its own. Moholy once captured, in a chance snapshot, the dominating position of the viewer and the photographer (cf. pl. 5). Mutual penetration and superimposition of two or more autonomous systems are among the chief methods used by Moholy in his approach to photographic composition.

The oblique view from above: photographic counter-composition
Another system of forms is automatically superimposed on oblique shots taken from above. The

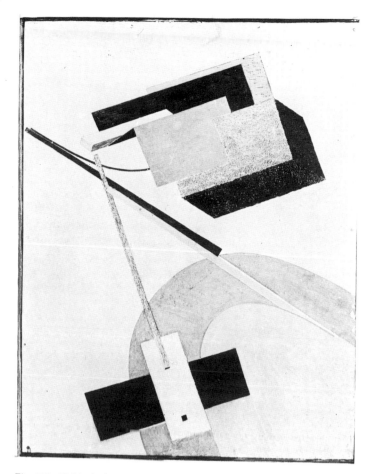

Fig. 25 El Lissitzky, *Proun*, 1920/21.

classicist and pre-fascist ideologies. From 1924 onwards the Surrealists began in Paris a more clearly defined struggle against these conservative and repressive concepts of order, by elaborating aesthetic techniques which placed spirit and nature in dialectical opposition to each other. Certainly, van Doesburg did not take up a position against nature as such, but rather against a fatalistic way of treating as nature the human spirit and intelligence. Evidently this was his reason for enlarging his concept of De Stijl and for putting 'nature' (in which he also included the purposefulness of architecture) and 'spirit' in active opposition to each other.

'The new painting can still have significance as a means of spiritual expression only in so far as it opposes natural organic structure to architectural structure instead of being homogeneous with it. Now this homogeneity was expressed by the exclusively horizontal-vertical [H.V.] determined painting in the H.V.-determined structure of architecture . . . In contrast painting (counter-composition) this extension of line and colour plane runs counter to the natural and architectural structure, i.e. contrasts with the latter.'[108]

Van Doesburg called this form of art 'elementarism' which 'through the suppression of a rigid state, arouses in us a new spiritual movement, accompanied by a new optics.'[109] Elementarism 'wishes to strengthen and arouse a spirit of opposition and revolt in the new generation and counts upon making possible . . . a real inner renewal of our mentality. This agitation, which is psychological rather than political, demands a heroic spontaneity . . . The Elementarist is a spiritual rebel, an agitator who wantonly disturbs at the expense of his own peace, the peace of the regularity

movements they have become more or less technical. Instinct has been mechanized. Our spirit plays no part in it. Our *spirit*, in so far as it has not become fossilized in our physical life, opposes this natural 'mechanism' and assumes a completely new dimension. We already more or less despise those who function organically in complete naturalness. This contempt is directed chiefly towards the complete identification with organic nature. What we miss in "natural" man is: opposition, contrast, resistance, struggle — in a word, "spirit".'[106] Van Doesburg even designated the *equilibrium* between nature and spirit as a 'dead point'. 'If this equilibrium were a new construction or plasticism, it could neither be improved nor developed. The equilibrium achieved would, in this instance, be absolute instead of relative, stable instead of labile; it would be eternal and unchangeable.'[107] Dada had already tried, with a leap of irony, to escape from the horrible prospect that had been opened up with renewed strength at that time, by

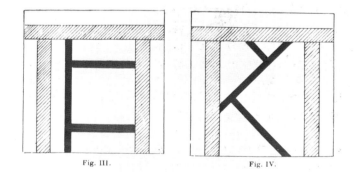

Fig. III.   Fig. IV.

Fig. 26 Theo van Doesburg, *Classical and counter-composition*, 1928.

33

and repetitiveness of bourgeois life . . . The Elementarist opposes to this uniformity the absolute concept of universal movement. It even includes his personal ego. Thus . . . consciousness as a product or goal of life occupies an elementary position (fulfilment of consciousness).'[110]

Here one can sense the closeness to Surrealism, and also the affinity to Moholy. Van Doesburg realized his ideas artistically in a curiously abstract way in some of his counter-compositions. Moholy's photographs, on the contrary, show an application of van Doesburg's ideas that is more related to reality; these photographs, especially those bird's-eye views taken by Moholy, may even have influenced van Doesburg's 'counter'-concept, though it is hard to establish this now. However, Moholy and van Doesburg had been in touch a short time before (in 1925) in Paris when van Doesburg had induced Moholy and Sigfried Giedion and their respective wives to spend a holiday on the island of Belle-Ile-en-Mer, off Brittany, the natural beauty of which he had first got to know the previous year.[111] The friends' acceptance of this idea may prove that the avant-garde, conscious as it was of technology, in no way hated nature as such, only the sentimental bourgeois attitude to nature; this they regarded as a form of romanticism which sought to tie the intellect to the emotions.

During his stay on Belle-Ile-en-Mer in 1925, Moholy seemed to pass through a significant phase in his photography. Sigfried Giedion has described it thus: 'I remember a holiday spent together on Belle-Ile-en-Mer where Moholy, deliberately ignoring the usual standpoint of a photographer, took shots looking up from below and looking down from above. The surprising foreshortenings and plunging lines were, only a few years later, to find universal favour as being artistically attractive.'[112] It is certain that Moholy had got to know similar photographic procedures through Mayakovsky and Rodchenko.[113] Perhaps he had even seen performances of Dziga Vertov's film *Kino-Auge* ('Cinema Eye') which had been awarded a prize at the Art-Deco Exhibition.[114] In 1925, in the original edition of his own book *Painting Photography Film*, Moholy had already mentioned the potential of film to achieve 'super-reality' (i.e. to go beyond reality) in an altogether surrealist sense as 'combination, projection of images on top of one another and side by side; penetration; super-reality . . .'.[115]

If we once more briefly look back to the 'counter-composition' of van Doesburg, Moholy's parallel in photography (fig. 27) shows consequences of its own. The counter-composition (fig. 28) is deliberately arranged in a diagonal relationship to natural architectural space; it seems to liberate itself and to 'fly'. In the photograph the impression is the reverse: the rectangle of the picture is superimposed on the system of diagonal co-ordinates of the picture-subject and evokes the impression that the viewer is 'flying'. However, because the viewer stands firm and in a vertical position in real space, the pictures achieve sometimes within themselves stubborn energies of motion that strike the viewer as 'objective'. This autonomy of objects which is the result of photographic counter-composition, together with the aspect of the 'haptic' reality of the elements, easily leads to an impression of bizarre

Fig. 27 L. Moholy-Nagy, Untitled, 1925(?).

34

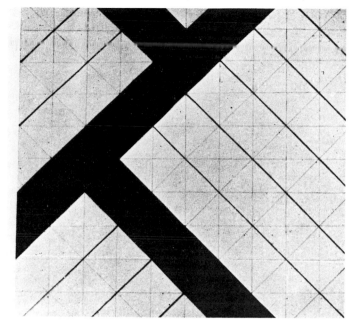

Fig. 28 Theo van Doesburg, *Counter-composition*, 1925.

movement and fantastic appearances. Moholy accepted, even intended, this latent surrealism, as is shown by several of his photographs (cf. pl. 41).

In fig. 29 the 'observation' post alienates the natural relationships: one woman, in fact lying on the deck, seems to be standing, the other one to be

Fig. 29 L. Moholy-Nagy, Untitled, n.d.

sitting on the rail, and from the left a curious 'rope-face' is angled towards them — a charming, surrealist piece of 'holiday humour'.

From 'dialectical' to 'organic' manipulation

As a result of this attitude to observation, one senses in all of Moholy's photographs a 'dialectic' distance from automatic procedures, a partly formal, partly also ironical isolation of the subject from the interaction of objects to the point of a 'higher' insight. In the course of time this attitude changes in character: the presentations of interaction which initially had been 'open' and, in a Constructivist sense, could still be 'entered', now become hermetically closed, complex interwoven figures.

The replacement of dynamic and constructive systems by systems of pictures which tend to be integrated was already latent in Moholy's paintings when he first began to apply the principles of overlapping and transparency. These procedures which Moholy described later on as 'super-imposition',[116] in the cinematic sense of mixing images, lend to the picture elements the character of being interactive and interwoven. The viewer is not 'harnessed' to them but rather he may be aesthetically involved in them in such a way that he seems to experience intuitively a 'fruitful' moment of transition. The concept of tension which strongly characterized Moholy's painting in the 1920s disappears in the course of the 1930s and gives place — above all in the U.S.A. — to an even more intricate interweaving of curved planes and lines in space. The last works of this kind Moholy called 'space modulators'. They are sculptures in Plexiglass which grow on all sides through space in fluidly curved planes and appear, in their reflections and transparent shadows, to bend and twist space itself.

This modulation (cf. p. 24), too, is based on Moholy's principle of the interaction of two systems (cf. p. 32). The similarity of *space* and *light* as 'substances', which was one of Moholy's early ideas, is taken here to its logical extreme.[118]

The portrait of 'Ellen' (1929; cf. pl. 70) could be described as the photographic predecessor of a space modulator. It is the product of transferring the principle of interaction to very closely related systems and their increasing contact with light. The 'system' of the blades of grass is projected on to the body lying behind it, the form of the human body *modulates* the projection of shadows whereby the to the subject new forms of participation; such participation, seen as an 'insight', was to acquire a creative role. For this reason Moholy stressed the 'objectivity' of the camera picture — not, to be sure, in the picture as a whole, but in its 'elementary' form — and rejected the customary associations of visual perception with perspective. For this reason he became enthusiastic, experiencing the true joy of discovery, about the capacity of photography to register phenomena 'automatically'. There exists a characteristic description by Beaumont Newhall: 'What separates him [Moholy], however, from the straight photographer is that he discovered beauty

Fig. 31 L. Moholy-Nagy, *Inverted curve*, moulded Plexiglass sheet, 1946.

Fig. 30 L. Moholy-Nagy, *Ellen*, 1928.

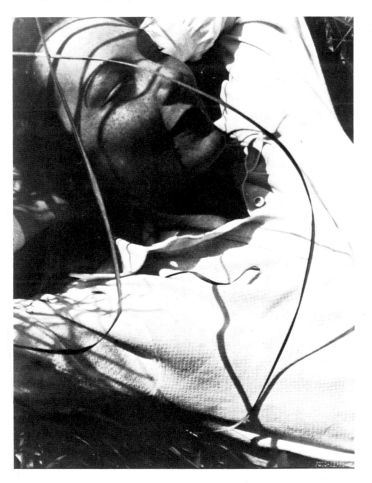

'constellation' of objects enters into a tightly interwoven interaction in space. What is individual (the human figure) modulates what is general (the grassy environment) and in this way the latter, too, achieves individuality. The agent of this procedure is light. The particular 'meaning' in this example might be that the individual phenomenon only becomes manifest when it 'modulates' the general one. The individual phenomenon becomes a special case of the general; it is the synthetic result of the interaction of elements which, in the first instance, were unconnected. Only photography, with its equality of elements and its 'automatic' fixation of otherwise undiscovered constellations in space, could have hit on such a model of perception. Through photography the Constructivist, conditioned as he was to perceive tensions in space, could become aware of the 'autonomous' dialectic of external motion, and through this insight, of the necessity of opening up

after the photograph had been taken, and it did not matter to him who made the photograph or why it had been made. Once, looking at a photograph which he had taken years previously from a bridge tower at Marseilles, his attention was held as if it were a new thing and the work of another. "What a powerful form!", he said, pointing at a coiled-up rope. "I never saw it before." It was this attitude of approaching photographs that led him to appreciate scientific photographs for their quite often accidental beauty.'[119] (This quotation relates to pl. 47.)

The anecdote shows Moholy's joy in discovery when it was a question of plucking aspects of 'individual' phenomena from the continuity of innumerable automatic procedures and thus of securing for the perceiving subject an individual place in this continuum.

The fascination with the automatism of internal and external processes provides a connecting link between belief in technology and Surrealism. However, the physiognomy of the 'automatic procedures', drawn up by Moholy, remains almost always in low key; it never becomes, as with the Surrealists, an obsession with 'actual' reality. He regards everything instinctive and natural as a sort of fate which has to be overcome: for instance, in his description of the relations between the sexes, which occurs in his second filmscript, *Once a Chicken, Always a Chicken* ('Huhn bleibt Huhn').[120] Properly understood, this piece contains a rather grim critique of human behaviour viewed as a purely functional, behaviourist mechanism governed by stimulus and reaction.

At times fate appears to be simply an involuntarily comic aspect of the human species – frequently so in photomontages like *Das Weltgebäude* ('The structure of the world'; fig. 32). The galaxy of women's legs reminds one of Raoul Hausmann's sarcastic counsel: 'Germans may be well advised to occupy themselves first of all with a systematic division of a soup with dumplings into dumplings and soup – otherwise they will never transcend women's legs which look like sausages, plans for the domination of the world, and Expressionism, i.e. a culture of mendacious stupidity.'[121] Moholy's ideal was independence of and freedom from restraint, from the 'cloddishness' of all things human.[122]

The special character of reality in Moholy's photography seems to lie in his own ability to achieve this freedom from restraint and the domination of the subject in his photographs; however, he achieves this in the specific form of the definition of the subject arising out of the objectivity of things – a mixture of the awareness of an old bohemian with a new, positive interest in the concreteness of the world. In terms of the history of ideas one can recognize in the manipulation of elements an almost violent re-interpretation on the part of Moholy of the old naturalistic theory of cognition which defined the human person as a mere 'impersonal happening',

Fig. 32 L. Moholy-Nagy, *The structure of the world*, photomontage, 1925.

as something 'shifted around that was not the master over his own decisions but something repeatedly moved away from the centre of his own will by "inexplicable" forces and thereby changed into a sort of machine'.[123] Moholy, too, subscribed to a school of thought called activism, which protested against this mechanization of the mind[124] and pleaded for its creative involvement of the subjective spirit in the material processes of the world. Paul Citroen described Moholy's subjective creative involvement in external circumstances: 'The processes of living, from eating and drinking and sleeping to a streetcar ride or a business meeting, were as much part of his work as giving a lecture or painting a picture. The mere fact of existence implied a continuous process of growth, in which positive and negative factors were analysed through observation and experimentation, and added to his creative stock.'[125] Citroen had been a Dadaist, and it is striking that he described Moholy's life from the point of view of the Dadaist ideal.

However, Moholy's second wife and biographer, Sibyl Moholy-Nagy, writing somewhat later, saw in Moholy's attitude merely an expression of the principle of integration[126] of the essentially amateurish manner of working of an artist who wanted to achieve the total solution of the most diverse tasks by personal dedication.

In such notions of a harmonious integration one readily detects the influence of the pragmatic doctrine of the American philosopher John Dewey who looked on human behaviour as, above all, biological and functional rather than truly comprehending. On the other hand we have to bear in mind that in the transition from bourgeois empirical criticism to American pragmatism, Moholy remained faithful for several years at least to the fruitful position of activism because it was dialectical, more demanding and exposed to constant contradictions. These same years, from the beginning of the 1920s to the beginning of the 1930s, constitute, in fact, Moholy's photographic decade.

Nothing shows better the attitude of the artist moving from that of a bohemian outsider to the position of activism than does Moholy's photography, with its revealing treatment of the subject. Its most significant characteristic seems to be that it was done, for the most part, on journeys. The freedom of the traveller, his kinetic relationship to static places, manifests itself in the easy-going, holiday atmosphere suggested by many of Moholy's photographs. It is striking that they never show a local sight or reveal the aura of a place. At best one may discover largely by chance where they were taken. They owe their existence to the stimulation provided by the subject in a foreign environment and his unprejudiced attitude towards 'new' visual material. In the last analysis the central feature of the photographs is not the subject but Moholy the traveller who documents himself in the course of his travels. In an age of cheerless educational journeyings to view the aura that surrounds world-famous sites, this sort of travel photography provided a real liberation from the dead weight of bourgeois conventions.

The ever more frequent bird's-eye views in these travel pictures are the best witnesses to this euphoria

Fig. 33 Chermayev, L. Moholy-Nagy, about 1928.

of liberation. Moreover, they show directly a truly spectacular negation of the traditional concept of material work as the basis of all commitment and true worth.

However, this holiday-like, freely floating aspect of Moholy's photography is not simply a Sunday photographer's escape from the everyday world, but an attempt to raise the subjective 'manipulation' of experienced reality to the level of the category of non-alienated human 'work' — of the aesthetic employment of the total environment for human 'use'. In this way, art — in the sense in which it had been discussed in various ways in the 1920s — is no longer 'representational' or 'narrative' but 'productive'; it defines the position of the subject by means of the object.

Moholy, too, who separated what is conditional on time from the 'elemental', was interested in making manifest the generally human aspect within the all-powerful purposefulness of the historical and concrete moment which is the raw material of photographic manipulation. But this work became ever more strongly a kind of 'blocked account' for a future 'collective' society which was Moholy's romantic dream. A person like El Lissitzky had long since resigned himself to such a situation; in 1925 he wrote: 'Nobody is the slightest bit concerned where works of art land up today. Nobody cares two hoots if snobbery is greater than ever. One should keep them safely stowed away: for the things which are coming to life now will have their day.'[127]

Moholy, on the contrary, regarded any recognition from within established society as a victory, even at the price of ever more frequent compromises — as later on in exile — and of avoiding controversy.

Almost remote in style is one of his later photographs, taken in Chicago (cf. pl. 106), in which he sought once more to produce the spirit of his early pictures of the radio towers in Berlin (pls. 39, 40). But what earlier on had been an 'arabesque', its farcical quality tempered by the projection of shadows and dominated by the intellect, has now

become a sinister configuration — undialectic, organic, of necessity nature-like, 'existentialist' in so far as the alienated environment as such becomes the reason for self-enjoyment. For the first time there manifests itself 'empathy' with the alien automatism — and this in so far-reaching a manner that Moholy even transformed the tracks of people crossing the street into a 'peinture de geste' of its own. In this irrational and magical procedure Moholy abandoned completely the subversive content of his earlier filmscript *Dynamic of the Metropolis* and substituted for it signs of fatalism. Here in fact is to be found the

Fig. 35 L. Moholy-Nagy, *Linear mobility*, drawing, 1938.

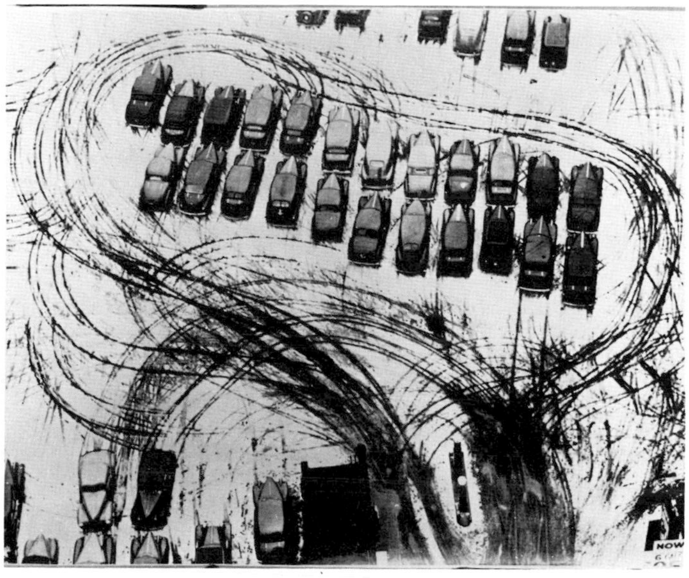

Fig. 34 L. Moholy-Nagy, *Parking lot in winter*, Chicago, 1938.

true germ of the 'subjective' photography of the 1950s which harks back to photographs like Moholy's *Parking lot* (fig. 34) for its legitimation, but this must not be regarded as Moholy's sole photographic legacy.

39

NOTES ON THE TEXT

1 E.g., B. Marilies von Brevern, *Künstlerische Photographie von Hill bis Moholy-Nagy*, vol. 15 in the series 'Bilderhefte der Museen Preußischer Kulturbesitz', Berlin 1972.

2 See Moholy's widely disseminated essay 'Photographie ist Lichtgestaltung' ('Photography is Manipulation of Light'), in *Photographische Korrespondenz*, 1 May 1928, slightly adapted from the original version published in *Bauhaus* (1928), 1, pp. 2ff., under the title 'fotografie ist lichtgestaltung'. For translation see Appendix, pp. 47ff.

3 In an address given at the Galerie Hans Goltz, Munich, in 1929; for a report see *Das Kunstblatt* 1929, p. 157.

4 E.g., in a letter to Gropius in 1935 (see Appendix, p. 51); in 1936 Moholy's friend Sigfried Giedion laid great emphasis on his 'fundamental painterly approach' (*Telehor*, special Moholy-Nagy number, p. 116); cf. also Moholy's own description of himself – 'I am 34 years old and am a painter' – in his contribution on photography in H. and B. Rasch, *Gefesselter Blick, 25 kurze Monografien und Beiträge über neue Werbegestaltung*, Stuttgart 1930.

5 Cf. Winfried Ranke, 'Zur sozialdokumentarischen Fotografie um 1900', in *Kritische Berichte* published by the Verein für Kunst- und Kulturwissenschaft, Ulm (1977, nos. 2/3), pp. 5–36.

6 See the works and impulses of Richard Hiepe in the journal *Tendenzen*, and Eckhard Siepmann, *Montage John Heartfield*, Berlin 1977.

7 Herbert Molderings, 'Überlegungen zur Fotografie der Neuen Sachlichkeit und des Bauhauses', in *Kritische Berichte* (cf. note 5), p. 83.

8 Following Bertolt Brecht's statement: 'A photograph of the Krupp factory or of AEG reveals almost nothing about these institutions. The essential reality has slid into the functional.'; see Walter Benjamin, *Das Kunstwerk im Zeitalter seiner Kunstsoziologie*, Frankfurt/Main 1963, pp. 90f. (originally published in the same author's *Kleine Geschichte der Photographie*, 1931).

9 *Malerei Photographie Film* (Bauhaus Book, no. 8), 1925, p. 29; English edition *Painting Photography Film*, 1969, p. 35 (cf. Bibliography, below).

10 *De Stijl* IV (1921), no. 10.

11 Reproduced in E. Siepmann, op. cit. (cf. note 6), p. 43, in the article by Hanne Bergius, 'Zur Wahrnehmung und Wahrnehmungskritik in der dadaistischen Phase von Grosz und Heartfield'.

12 In collaboration with Hanne Bergius; in Karl Riha (ed.), *Dada Berlin, Texte, Manifeste und Aktionen*, Stuttgart 1977 p. 29.

13 Ibid.

14 Raoul Hausmann, 'PREsentismus – gegen den Puffkeismus der teutschen Seele', first published in *De Stijl*, September 1921; reprinted in Raoul Hausmann, *Am Anfang war Dada* (ed. Karl Riha and Günter Kampf), Gießen 1972.

15 Ibid.

16 Printed as an appendix to *Malerei Photographie Film* (also in English edition; cf. note 9); on its background see also note 74.

17 Op. cit.; English ed., p. 130.

18 Lucia Moholy, *Marginalien zu Moholy-Nagy/Moholy-Nagy, Marginal Notes* (bilingual edition), Krefeld 1972.

19 Sophie Lissitzky-Küppers, *El Lissitzky, Maler, Architekt, Typograf, Fotograf*, Dresden 1967, p. 22; English edition, *El Lissitzky: Life. Letters. Texts*, London and Greenwich, Conn. 1968, p. 26.

20 László Moholy-Nagy, 'geradlinigkeit des geistes – umwege der technik', in *Bauhaus* I/1 (1926); English translation in R. Kostelanetz (ed.), *Moholy-Nagy*, New York 1970 and London 1971, pp. 187f.

21 Today, part of the modern psychological theory of perception intensifies the diagnosis of this situation with materialistic overtones; cf., for example, Klaus Holzkamp, *Sinnliche Erkenntnis, Historischer Ursprung und Gesellschaftliche Funktion der Wahrnehmung*, Frankfurt/Main 1973, pp. 332ff. Thus biological-sensual perception is no longer in a position to penetrate the illusory nature, pseudo-concreteness, and the contradictions of real situations.

22 In the journal *Bauhaus* (1928). Possibly the original title seemed too reminiscent of Art Nouveau, for the eight-volume work by Lothar von Kunovsky had the general title *Durch Kunst zu Leben* ('Through Art to Life'); the fifth volume – *Licht und Helligkeit* ('Light and Luminosity'), Jena 1906 – is a basic source of 'light visions' in the manner in which Moholy employed them. Kunovsky (p. 52) wrote: 'We should not be deterred from imagining a time when the artist seizes on the concave mirror, prisms and all kinds of polished apparatus which force sunlight to reveal purest colour; I see magical pictures in such colours, projected high in the sky.' Moholy wrote: 'I dreamed of light-apparatus, which might be controlled, either by hand or by an automatic mechanism, by means of which it would be possible to produce visions of light, in the air, in large rooms, on screens of unusual nature, on fog, vapor and clouds.' ('Light Architecture', *Industrial Arts*, I/1, 1936; reprinted in R. Kostelanetz [ed.], op. cit., pp. 155ff.). For Kunovsky, who speaks mainly in terms of the sun, 'light' was especially the means to the reintegration of human sensuality into the life of nature; Moholy's goal, on the other hand, was to generate new possibilities in the realm of optical designs and experiences, using modern technical lighting effects.

23 Cf. the sources in the Appendix, pp. 51f.

24 Cf. p. 39 and note 67. For Ostwald's initiatives, see his *Vorlesungen über Naturphilosophie, gehalten 1901*, 3rd ed., Leipzig 1905, pp. 447f.

25 Raoul Francé, *Bios — Die Gesetze der Welt* (various editions, e.g. Heilbronn 1922). Moholy cites this book explicitly for the first time in his *Vision in Motion* (1947). He had, however, previously used various ideas and terms derived from Francé's book, e.g. 'bios' (in *Von Material zu Architektur*, 1929, p. 177; cf. English ed., p. 46) and 'weltregelnde gesetze . . .' (op. cit., p. 189) = ' . . . laws to which man is subject' (English ed., p. 53). He also quotes *in extenso* (op. cit., p. 60; English ed., p. 29) Francé's proposals for 'bio-technics' as a method of research.

26 Paul Lindner, *Photographie ohne Kamera*, Berlin 1920, p. 54.

27 *Das Buch der Erfindungen, Gewerbe und Industrien*, 9th ed., X, pp. 368, 378.

28 Letter from Albert Einstein to A. Sommerfeld, dated 6 September 1920; printed in *Bild der Wissenschaft*, September 1977, p. 115.

29 See the catalogue of the exhibition 'Schadographien 1918–1975. Photogramme von Christian Schad', at the Von der Heydt Museum, Wuppertal (Feb.–March 1975).

30 Man Ray, *Self Portrait*, London 1963, pp. 128–9.

31 Richard Huelsenbeck, *Dr. Billig am Ende*, 1921; printed in *Dada, eine literarische Dokumentation* (ed. Huelsenbeck), Reinbek 1964, p. 163.

32 Cf. Appendix below, pp. 51f.

33 'Photographie ist Lichtgestaltung', op. cit., p. 134 (cf. note 2).

34 See 'Light — a Medium of Plastic Expression', in *Broom*, March 1923; also in R. Kostelanetz (ed.), op. cit., pp. 117f.

35 Cf. p. 21 and note 50.

36 Cf. 'Abstract of an Artist', in *The New Vision*, 4th ed., 1949, p. 75.

37 *Malerei Photographie Film* (op. cit.; cf. note 9), pp. 26f.; English ed., pp. 33f.

38 Herwarth Walden, 'Technik und Kunst', in *Der Sturm* (1921).

39 In adopting the term 'photogram' Moholy wanted to suggest an analogy with the idea of information being automatically transmitted, as expressed in the word 'telegram'; see his letter to Gropius, p. 51.

40 J. Meier-Graefe, *Paul Cézanne*, 3rd ed., Munich 1910, p. 14.

41 For the influence of Schwitters's *Merz*-pictures on Moholy's discovery of the technique for producing

photograms, see *The New Vision*, 4th ed., 1949, p. 72.

42 The Schwitters quotation (from *MERZ*, I, 1923) is taken from Sibyl Moholy-Nagy, *Experiment in Totality*, p. 24.

43 R. Hausmann, 'PREsentismus . . .', op. cit. (cf. note 14).

44 R. Hausmann, 'Kurt Schwitters wird Merz', in *Am Anfang war Dada* (cf. note 14).

45 'Dadaism is . . . a tactile attitude which rejects points of view that clearly show a lack of life, without in any way wishing to change the world in principle.' – R. Hausmann, 'Dada ist mehr als Dada', 1921; cf. R. Huelsenbeck (ed.), *Dada, eine literarische Dokumentation*, Reinbek 1964, p. 39.

46 'Abstract of an Artist', in *The New Vision*, 4th ed., 1949, p. 79.

47 Ibid.

48 Letter of 1927, quoted in W. Haftmann's Introduction to K. Malewitsch [Malevich], *Suprematismus ı Die gegenstandlose Welt* (trans. Hans von Riesen), Cologne 1962, p. 22.

49 In 1926 (cf. note 20).

50 From an advertisement in *Offset*, vol. 7 (1926), p. 389.

51 'Photographie ist Lichtgestaltung', op. cit.; cf. note 2 and Appendix, pp. 47ff.

52 L. Schreyer, 'Anschauung und Gleichnis – Die Gegenwart der Kunst', in *Der Sturm*, June 1923, p. 92.

53 E.g., *Malerei Photographie Film* (cf. note 9), p. 26; English ed., p. 33.

54 Ibid.

55 Op. cit., pp. 18, 31; English ed., pp. 21, 40.

56 Op. cit., p. 115; English ed., p. 123.

57 I. Meidner, 'Anweisung zum Malen von Großstadtbildern'; cited in Dieter Schmidt, *Manifeste Manifeste*, Dresden 1964, pp. 84ff.

58 *Malerei Photographie Film* (cf. note 9), pp. 118–21; English ed., pp. 126f.

59 Cf. note 50.

60 In hints on photographic procedure published in *Führer V.D.A.V.* (Verband Deutscher Amateurphotographenvereine), Berlin 1927, p. 20.

61 *Malerei Photographie Film* (cf. note 9), p. 115; English ed., p. 122.

62 Op. cit., p. 114; English ed., p. 122.

63 Op. cit., p. 6; English ed., p. 9.

64 Cf. Sibyl Moholy-Nagy's report in *Experiment in Totality*, pp. 60ff.

65 'Probleme des neuen Films', in *Die Form*, 5 (1932).

66 W. Kandinsky, *Point and Line to Plane*, New York 1947, pp. 144f.; originally published as Bauhaus Book no. 9: *Punkt und Linie zu Fläche*, Munich 1926.

67 *Malerei fotografie film* (1927), p. 23; English ed., p. 25 (cf. note 9).

68 László Moholy-Nagy and Alfred Kemény, 'The Dynamic Constructive System of Forces'; originally appeared as 'Dynamisches-Konstruktivisches Kräftesystem' in *Der Sturm*, no. 12 (1922) – cf. note 101. The English version appears in *Vision in Motion*, 1947, p. 238; cf. also R. Kostelanetz (ed.), op. cit., p. 29. The words quoted are probably Kemény's; he had first discussed these ideas with artists in Russia and had returned to Germany not long before. He set out his own thoughts in an article in *Der Sturm*, no. 14, April 1923, pp. 62ff. ('Das dynamische Prinzip der Weltkonstruktion'). This article combines and concentrates the arguments put forward in two separate publications of 1922: Moholy's own 'Produktion – Reproduktion' (cf. Appendix, pp. 46f.), and Moholy/Kemény's 'Dynamisches-Konstruktivisches Kräftesystem'.

69 'Stattliches Bauhaus in Weimar 1919–23', published by Verlag Albert Langen, Munich 1923, p. 140.

70 *Malerei Photographie Film* (cf. note 9), p. 37; English ed., p. 28.

71 Ibid.

72 *Malerei fotografie film* (1927; cf. note 9), p. 26; English ed., p. 28.

73 Op. cit., p. 22; English ed., p. 29.

74 *Malerei Photographie Film*, p. 22. This typophoto of the filmscript cannot be earlier than 1924/5, because in Moholy's work (p. 121) he uses a photograph taken by Erich Mendelsohn in New York in the autumn of 1924; the photo appears as fig. 25 in Mendelsohn's *Amerika*, Berlin 1926.

75 See *Von Material zu Architektur*, p. 72; also English ed., with revised text, p. 32. In 1923 Alfred Kemény had written in *Der Sturm*: 'Constructivity is . . . one of the principal laws both of cosmic and of human structure [*Aufbau*; note the play on the German words *baut auf* and *Aufbau*]: Constructivity, which depends on dynamic opposites of contrasting movements . . . Therein lies the ethical value of constructive – inventive – work, especially in that through it there will always be aroused a feeling of the inferiority of the agent and that from this will result an enrichment of the possibilities of organic function . . . We must now examine, in the context of fine art, these new active laws of constructive design which actively enrich given functional situations of the human organism.' Cf. note 68.

76 *Von Material zu Architektur*, p. 186; English ed., p. 51.

77 Ibid.

78 Op. cit., p. 187; English ed., p. 52.

79 Op. cit., p. 37, fig. 19; not in English ed.

80 Op. cit., p. 41, fig. 23; English ed., p. 26, fig. 4. Cf. also my note to pl. 99, below. As early as 1888 Ernst Mach wrote in an article, apropos the scientific applications of photography: 'Should not the time-lapse principle also be of value? . . . Pictures of a man, from the cradle onwards . . . to his decline in old age, presented in this way in the space of a few seconds, ought to have a great aesthetic and ethical impact. There can be little doubt that new insights would be stimulated in this way.'; see *Populärwissenschaftliche Vorlesungen*, 4th ed., Leipzig 1910, pp. 134–5.

81 Cf. note 66: op. cit., p. 17.

82 This phrase is borrowed from Rainer Maria Rilke, who praised works of art as 'transcending' reality through the hand of man. Even Rilke, however, had earlier (in *Über den jungen Dichter*, 1913) imbued that very transcending of the aesthetic with scepticism.

83 Cf. R. Hamann and J. Hermand, *Naturalismus*, Berlin 1959, pp. 143ff., and 203ff.

84 In the exaggerated phrasing of Alfred Kemény, this development is described thus: 'The artistic trends following cubism – Suprematism and Constructivism – emphasized for the first time in fine art the rigid organization of the human situation: construction as a primary productive, and not as a secondary reproductive, means of creative work . . . The transformation of the potential energy of a work of art into an intense psychic agitation gives – in contrast to the decadence, based simply on fine shades of meaning and distinctions, of bourgeois culture – the original consciousness of dynamic constructivity, the feeling of a firm combination of contrasting dynamic legitimacy, as man's highest form of energy-perception by which the world is no longer experienced in countless fine gradations, but in the most powerful and original contrasts of its dynamic dialectic.' Cf. note 68.

85 In an article, translated from the German by P. Morton Shand, entitled 'How Photography Revolutionises Vision', in *The Listener*, 8 November 1933.

86 W. Benjamin, op. cit. (cf. note 8), pp. 46ff.; for Benjamin's connections with Riegl, see W. Kemp, *Walter Benjamin und die Kunstgeschichte*, part 1: 'Benjamins Beziehungen zur Wiener Schule', in *Kritische Berichte* published by the Verein für Kunst- und Kulturgeschichte, Ulm (1973, no. 3), pp. 30–51.

87 For a discussion of visual and haptic perception and its significance in art, see D. Brothwell (ed.), *Beyond Aesthetics*, London 1976, pp. 130ff.

88 *Von Material zu Architektur*, p. 18; English ed., p. 19.

89 Ibid.

90 Op. cit., p. 222; English ed., p. 64.

91 Cf. *Malerei Photographie Film*, p. 18; English ed., pp. 23f.

92 Cf. p. 27 and note 85.

93 *Von Material zu Architektur*, p. 33; English ed., p. 26. To date no research has been undertaken on the history of the concept of 'Faktur' (= 'surface aspect' or 'surface treatment', showing the method of production). Moholy's application of the term is a variation on that of the terminology introduced by the Russian Constructivists. In 1924 Henryk Berlewi, in an article entitled 'Mechano-Faktur', proposed the use of a limited range of mechanically derived stereotypes as equivalents of the chaotic multitude of treatments of material surfaces used in both natural and craft contexts; almost a mechanized Cézanne. Moholy's adaptation of the most varied types of surfaces as photographic 'light'-equivalents indicates a further step in this process of standardization.

94 *Von Material zu Architektur*, p. 178; not in English ed.

95 Op. cit., figs. 81, 82, 98, 168; in the English edition many of the illustrations were omitted or in some cases substitutes inserted – cf. pp. 43f., fig. 21.

96 Op. cit., fig. 152; English ed., fig. 30.

97 Op. cit., p. 167; English ed., p. 47.

98 The term was introduced into the language of aesthetics by Riegl; cf. *Die spätrömische Kunstindustrie*, vol. 1, 1901. The concept of 'Kunstwollen', although frequently referred to in modern writing, here applies only to the ideas prevailing in the 1920s. Moholy's use of the term 'Ausdruckswunsch' ('planned expression'), which occurs in *Von Material zu Architektur*, p. 21 (English ed., p. 23), is closely related to Riegl's 'Kunstwollen' (which term was also used by Walter Gropius in a theoretical sense). See E. Panovsky, 'Der Begriff des Kunstwollens', in *Zeitschrift für Ästhetik und allgemeine Wissenschaft*, 14 (1920), pp. 321ff.; also Kurt Badt, *Raumphantasien und Raumillusionen*, Cologne 1963.

99 *Von Material zu Architektur*, p. 195; English ed., p. 57.

100 *Von Material zu Architektur*, p. 195; English ed., pp. 49f. Cf. S. Giedion's observations on space in the note to pl. 41, below.

101 First printed in *Der Sturm*, 12 (1922) and quoted in part in *Von Material zu Architektur* (1929). In the latter, on p. 162, Moholy suggested amending the phrase 'dynamic-constructive' to read 'kinetic-constructive'; also, in the penultimate sentence quoted here, the word 'man' ('mensch') was introduced in the 1929 version. Cf. *The New Vision*, pp. 49f., and *Vision in Motion*, p. 238; another (complete) translation may be found in R. Kostelanetz (ed.), op. cit., p. 29.

102 El Lissitzky, 'Proun', in *De Stijl*, 1922.

103 For the concepts of 'activation' and 'dissection' see W. Benjamin, op. cit. (see note 8), p. 36. Alexander Rodchenko, in an article on the 'paths of modern photography' in the Russian journal *Novy Lef* (1928; no. 9, p. 39), wrote: 'One must take pictures of an object from different angles and under different conditions, viewing it as it were from all sides, and not just looking at it as through a keyhole.' See the catalogue of the exhibition '"Kunst in die Produktion", Sowjetische Kunst während der Phase der Kollektivierung und Industrialisierung 1927–1933', Berlin 1977, p. 85.

104 Cf. note 75.

105 R. Hausmann, 'Dada in Europa', in *Der Dada* 3, 1920, pp. 5ff.; cited in E. Siepmann, op. cit. (cf. note 6), p. 83.

106 Theo van Doesburg, 'Malerei – Von Komposition zu Kontra-Komposition', *De Stijl*, no. 73/74 (1926); English translation in Hans L. C. Jaffé, *De Stijl*, London and New York 1970, pp. 201ff., as 'Painting: From Composition to Counter-Composition'.

107 Jaffé, op. cit., p. 204.

108 Op. cit., p. 205.

109 See van Doesburg's fragment of a manifesto, 'Malerei und Plastik, Elementarismus', in *De Stijl*, no. 78 (1927); English translation in Jaffé, op. cit., pp. 213ff., as 'Painting and Sculpture: Elementarism (Fragment of a Manifesto)'.

110 Jaffé, op. cit., pp. 215ff.

111 Information from Dr Carola Giedion-Welcker of Zurich, in the course of a personal interview.

112 From S. Giedion's Preface in the special Moholy-Nagy number of *Telehor* (1936); cf. note to pl. 20, below.

113 Cf. pl. 86. For information concerning Moholy's contacts with Rodchenko and Mayakovsky I am indebted to Hubertus Gaßner.

114 Later, Sophie Küppers also reported on Dziga Vertov's films in *Das Kunstblatt*, 1929, pp. 141ff.; there, the première of *Kino-Auge* in Paris (1925) is mentioned on p. 142.

115 *Malerei Photographie Film*, p. 29; English ed., p. 35.

116 In his supplement (1935) to 'probleme des neuen films' (1928–30), in *Telehor*, p. 127; there, he declared that, in contrast to the 'machine-gun' montage of scenes in the silent film, in colour films superimposition ('I have used this technique for years in my paintings') 'facilitates the smooth transition from one scene to the next . . .'. For an English translation see R. Kostelanetz (ed.), op. cit., pp. 139ff.

117 At the time of his stay in London Moholy had already adopted 'organic' design principles, both in shop-window displays and in typography. In Sibyl Moholy-Nagy's *Experiment in Totality*, p. 123, we read: 'All his commercial design of that period reflected his predominant interest in contour, the flow of curved and crossed lines . . . Looking one night over typography and posters done during the Bauhaus years, Moholy said: "I was much too heavy-handed. The solid rectangular beams, the filled dots and black cubes are a mistake. They stress detail and distract the eye from the unity of the visual impression. A printed communication should be a whole. Neither violent color contrasts nor heavy typographical detail can achieve that. It's the line continuity that creates a visual entity."'

118 Cf. note to pl. 41, below.

119 Beaumont Newhall, *The History of Photography from 1839 to the present day*, 2nd ed., New York 1964, p. 163.

120 Written 1925–30, making use of a motif from Kurt Schwitters's 'Auguste Bolte'; English version printed in *Vision in Motion*, pp. 285ff., and in R. Kostelanetz (ed.), op. cit., pp. 124ff.

121 R. Hausmann, *Rückkehr zur Gegenständlichkeit der Kunst*, 1920; quoted in *Dada – eine literarische Dokumentation* (op. cit.; cf. note 45), p. 111.

122 Cf. *Dada – eine literarische Dokumentation* (op. cit.), p. 124, for Ernst Kallai's views on the 'ethics' of Constructivism; on p. 128 Hausmann speaks of the 'cloddishness of the German soul'.

123 R. Hamann and J. Hermand, op. cit. (cf. note 83), p. 206.

124 A concept occurring in the work of Walther Rathenau before the First World War; cf. his *Zur Mechanik des Geistes*, Berlin 1913.

125 Sibyl Moholy-Nagy, op. cit. (cf. note 64), p. 41.

126 Op. cit., p. 125.

127 S. Lissitzky-Küppers, op. cit. (cf. note 19), pp. 63f.; English ed., p. 66.

Sources of figures in the text

(for abbreviations see p. 60)

Fig. 2 Klihm Coll.

Fig. 3 Bildarchiv Foto Marburg (2A 3456/23).

Fig. 4 Smithsonian Institution, Washington, D.C.

Fig. 5 *Telehor* (1936).

Fig. 6 *Telehor* (1936).

Fig. 7 After G. Karginov, *Rodchenko* (English ed.), London and New York 1979, p. 66.

Fig. 8 Title page of *Der Sturm*, Berlin 1924.

Fig. 15 Illustrated in LM-N, *Von M zu A* (1929), p. 99 (not in English ed.), erroneously dated 1926; this dating also occurs in *De Stijl* (1927).

Fig. 16 LM-N, *MPF* (1925), p. 34; English ed., p. 42.

Fig. 17 LM-N, *Von M zu A* (1929), fig. 194 (not in English ed.); photo Weltspiegel.

Fig. 18 From *Der Arbeiterfotograf* (1928), 15, p. 6.

Fig. 19 Illustrated in Roh, no. 59.

Fig. 20 From *Novy Lef* (1929), no. 8–9, p. 65.

Fig. 21 Bauhaus-Archiv, Berlin.

Fig. 26 From *De Stijl* VII (1926), 73/74.

Fig. 28 From *De Stijl* VII (1927), 78.

Fig. 29 Levy Coll.

Fig. 31 From Sibyl M-N, *Experiment in Totality*, fig. 81.

Fig. 32 Illustrated in Roh, no. 58.

Fig. 35 After LM-N, *Vision in Motion* (1947), p. 36.

APPENDIX

A selection of original texts

Manifesto on Elemental Art

To the artists of the world!

We love bold invention, a renewal in art. Art is the product of all the forces of an epoch. We live in the present. Hence we demand the products of our epoch, we demand an art that can only originate from us, which did not exist before us and will not exist after us — that is not like changing fashion but the result of understanding that art is something new and does not stop at the products of the past. We stand for elemental art. Art is elemental because it does not philosophize, because it builds up its products from elements of its own. To yield to the elements of creativity means to be an artist. The elements of art cannot be determined by the artist alone. They do not originate in his individual and arbitrary will; the individual is not a separate unit and the artist is only an exponent of forces which make manifest the elements of the world. Artists, declare your solidarity with art! — Turn your backs on styles. We demand the abolition of style in order to achieve *style*! Style is never a plagiarism!

We regard this manifesto as a deed seized by the movement of our times. We announce through elemental art the renewal of our perception, of our consciousness of the indefatigable intersecting sources of energy which create the spirit and form of an epoch and with it art as something pure, liberated from utility and beauty, that allows something elemental to arise in the individual.

We demand elemental art! against the reactionary in art!

Berlin, Oct. 1921
R. Hausmann, Hans Arp, Ivan Puni, Moholy-Nagy

L. Moholy-Nagy:
Production — Reproduction

For a true understanding of the ways of expression and creativity in art and related (creative) fields, as well as for their development, it is necessary to investigate man himself and the means used by him in his creative activity.

The composition of a man is the synthesis of all his functional mechanisms, i.e. the man of a given period is most perfect when the functional mechanism of which he is composed — the cells as much as the complex organs — is being used to the limits of its biological capacity.

Art brings this about — and this is one of its most important missions, for the whole complex of effects depends upon the perfection of the functioning. Art attempts to establish far-reaching new relationships between the known and the as yet unknown optical, acoustical and other functional phenomena and compels their absorption by the functional apparatus. It is a basic fact of the human condition that the functional apparatus craves for further new impressions every time something new has been absorbed. That is the reason why new creative experiments are an enduring necessity. From this point of view, creations are valuable only when they produce new, previously unknown relationships. This is yet another way of saying that reproduction (the repetition of existing relationships), from the special point of view of creative art, can at best only be considered a matter of virtuosity.

Since production (productive creativity) is primarily of service to human development, we must endeavour to expand the apparatus (means) which has so far been used solely for purposes of reproduction for productive ends. This demands a thorough investigation on the basis of the following questions:

What purpose is served by this apparatus (means)?
What is its essential function?
Are we capable of expanding the apparatus so that it may serve production, and is it worth while?

We shall apply these questions to several examples: the gramophone; photography — the single (still) picture, and film.

The gramophone: until now the gramophone had the task of reproducing existing acoustical phenomena. The sound vibrations to be reproduced were scratched by a needle on a wax plate and were then transposed back into sound with the aid of a microphone. An expansion of the apparatus for production purposes might make it possible for scratches to be made in the wax plate by a person and without the aid of mechanical means. This sound when reproduced might result in acoustic effects which, without any new instruments and an orchestra, might signify a fundamental renewal in the production of sound (i.e. new, not yet existing sounds and sound-relationships) for the purposes of composition and the very concept of music itself.

46

Laboratory experiments are a basis for such work, i.e. the thorough investigation of the different kinds of sound vibrations produced by scratches, their different lengths, breadth, depth etc.; the investigation of self-produced scratches; and finally mechanical and technical experiments to perfect this kind of handwriting done by making scratches. (Eventually the mechanical reduction of large disks bearing such scratches.)

Photography. The photographic camera fixes light phenomena by means of a silver bromide plate placed at the back of the camera. Up till now we have used this capacity in a secondary sense only: for the fixation (reproduction) of single objects as they reflected light or absorbed it. If we desire a revaluation of this field, too, we must exploit the light-sensitivity of the silver bromide plate to receive and to fix upon it light phenomena (moments from light-displays) composed by ourselves with contrivances of mirrors or lenses etc.

For this, too, many experiments are needed: astronomical pictures (taken through telescopes) and X-ray pictures were interesting forerunners in this field.

Film. Mobile relationships of light projections. They are achieved by a series of sequences of fixed partial movements. Until now film production has limited itself in the main to the reproduction of dramatic actions. Doubtless, there exists in the field of film a whole number of important tasks; they are partly scientific (the dynamics of the different movements of people, animals, towns etc.; observations of different kinds, functional, chemical etc.; a film newspaper transmitted by wireless etc.; and partly, from a constructive point of view, the development of reproduction itself; however, the main task is the manipulation of motion as such. It is obvious that one cannot proceed to this without a self-produced play of forms as the agent of motion.

A naïve attempt in this direction was the trick-table (advertisements). Much more developed is the work of Ruttmann and the Clavilux[1] of Th. Wilfred which treated motion as dramatic action without objects (obstructions or as stylizations of erotic or natural events), though this was coupled with the attempt to incorporate a coloured picture.

The most perfect work of this kind up to date is that of Eggeling-Richter. Instead of dramatic action he already has a self-produced play of forms even if it still acts to the disadvantage of the manipulation of motion. For motion is still manipulated as such but too much stress is laid on the development of forms, actually to the point of almost totally absorbing the forces of motion. The way ahead lies in the manipulation of motion in space without dependence on a direct development of forms.
[Originally printed in *De Stijl* V, no. 7, July 1922, pp. 98–100]

---

[1] The name refers to a kind of colour organ, whereas here the Clavilux is a projection of light on to a plane, not into space.

L. Moholy-Nagy:
Photography is Manipulation of Light

The photographer is a manipulator of light, photography is manipulation of light.

If in photography the main point was not the changing play of light, until now hardly graspable by other means, but simply the question of the projection of objects in their formal appearance, we should then have to regard as good every flat, poorly lit and grey picture in which one could still recognize an object. However, nobody who has any understanding of photography would take such a view today.

This, then, is the first, most elementary piece of knowledge one has to acquire in order to manipulate a means for making pictures that has not yet been fully exploited. Above all, this knowledge is valid if one wants to take photographs without a camera, i.e. if we succeed in making use of the essence of photographic procedure, the potential of the light-sensitive layer, for purposes of composition.

It must be stressed that the essential tool of photographic procedure is not the camera but the light-sensitive layer. Specifically photographic laws and methods result from the reaction of this layer to light-effects which in their turn are influenced by the material, be it light or dark, smooth or rough.

Only after the problem has been investigated — i.e. in the second place — will one be able to examine the characteristic aspect of photography, as it has been understood up till now, viz. the connection between the light-sensitive layer and a camera obscura; and here also one will come to the conclusion that photography must not be confused with painting or drawing, that photography has a field of its own, with its own laws governing its means, and that the point is to make use of these laws and to develop them wherever possible.

Understanding is better served by the description of some practical experiments than by long theoretical explanations. These experiments can be divided into three groups:

1. the production of photographs without a camera, 'photograms', which result from the fixation of light-effects in gradations of black-white-grey directly on the photographic layer. The effect is sublime, radiant, almost dematerialized. In this way the potential of working with light is far more completely exploited than had previously been the case in painting. The contrasting relationships of the various graded values of grey, from the deepest black to the brightest white, that flow into each other, produce a penetrating light-effect which is without concrete significance, but is a direct optical experience for everyone.
2. the production of photographs with a camera obscura on the basis of new and extended laws.
3. the production of photomontages and photosculptures. Copying by superimposition; cutting and pasting; tricks.

1. Photography without a camera: the photogram

If one puts an object on sensitized paper and exposes it to the sun or to diffused daylight one can, within a short time, observe the formation of the contours of the object and its shadow in bright layers on a dark ground. One can achieve the same effect with paper sensitive to artificial light but with the difference that one cannot observe the progress of the formation of the picture as in the case of daylight-sensitive paper.

If one chooses a transparent or translucent object in place of an opaque one: crystal, glass, fluids, veils, nets, sieves etc., one gets, instead of the hard outlines, gradations of bright values. And if one combines these values or objects according to definite principles, the results will be clearer and richer, according to one's concentration and experience.

True, one can lay down rules for this work in outline only as it is a question of a hitherto unknown field of manipulation with a completely novel aspect of optical composition and, at the same time, a revaluation of traditional photography. Its essence is a never-failing certitude of feeling vis-à-vis the appearance of light — of its activity in brightness, of its passivity in the dark — its most delicate distribution of rays to the point of a perfect balance between the values of very small and very great tensions.

There is no possibility of a comparison with the material of other fields of composition. The laws of organization develop out of practical work, as the result of the human organism encountering newly discovered matter. So far experience teaches us that very subtle transitions can be of high intensity and that too strong contrasts of white and black weaken the effect.

A small quantity of white is capable of keeping in balance by its activity large areas of the deepest black and it is less a question of form than one of the quantity, direction and the positional relationships of the particular manifestations of light.

In addition one may note that photographs without a camera have in their negative aspect a wonderful softness of greys flowing into each other; whilst in their positive form — which can be also produced from paper negatives they result in harder, often pale values of grey. Their quite special character will only gradually come to be realized.

Experiments with photograms are of fundamental significance both for laymen and for professional photographers. They provide richer and more important insights into the meaning of the photographic procedure than do shots often taken quite mechanically with a camera. Here the organization of the light-effect is handled in a sovereign way, as it appears right to the manipulator, and independently of the limitations and chance nature of objects.

The light-sensitive layer — plate or paper — is a tabula rasa, a blank page on which one may make notes with light, just as the painter, working on his canvas in a sovereign way, uses his tools, brush and pigment.

Anybody who has once mastered the meaning of writing with light in producing photographs without a camera (photograms) will obviously also be able to work with a camera.

2. Photographs taken with a camera

The photographic apparatus has provided us with surprising possibilities which we are only now beginning to evaluate. These optical surprises latent in photographic procedure, become available to us very often through the chance results achieved by amateurs and through objective 'non-artistic' pictures taken by scientists, ethnographers etc. From them we have learnt a great deal about the specific and unique character of the photographic process and about the means photography puts at our disposal.

In the extension of the field of vision even the imperfect object of today is no longer confined to the narrow limits of our eyes. No manual means of manipulation (pencil, brush etc.) is capable of fixing segments of the environment seen in a similar fashion. It is equally impossible for either a craft tool or the eye to fix the essence of motion. The possibilities for distortion of objects — pictures normally regarded as rejects (worm's-eye view, bird's-eye view, and oblique view) — are not to be judged in a purely negative way, but rather provide us with an unprejudiced optical view which our eyes, bound as they are by laws of association, cannot give us.

And from another point of view: the subtlety of the effects of grey produces a result which can be just as sublime as that produced by the most enhanced colour tones.

By naming these fields, one is in no way suggesting the limits of the possibilities. Although photography is already more than a century old, it has only been possible in recent years, as the result of new developments, to look beyond the specific and see the consequences of manipulation. Only in the last few years have we become mature enough to understand these connections.

If we want to outline a programme for practical work on the basis of our so far still fragmentary knowledge, we must keep in mind, first of all, what is specifically photographic.

In the field of photography there is an enormous amount that remains hidden. In order to acquire the right finger-tip feel for the specific laws that govern its means, one must conduct practical experiments, including:

a) photographs of structures, textures, surface treatments with regard to their reaction to light (absorption, reflection, mirroring, dispersal effects etc.).

b) photographs in a so far unaccustomed style: rare views, oblique, upward, downward, distortions, shadow-effects, tonal contrasts, enlargements, micro-photographs.

c) photographs using a novel system of lenses, concave and convex mirrors, stereo-photographs on a disk etc.

The limits of photography are incalculable. Everything here is so new that the mere act of seeking leads by itself to creative results.

The oblivious pathfinder is technology. The illiterate of

the future will not be one who cannot write, but who does not know photography.

3. Photo-sculpture (photomontage)

Photomontage shows clearly how one can change imitative photographic procedure into purposeful, creative work.

Photomontage (photo-sculpture) goes back to the naïve, yet very skilful procedure of early photographers who produced a new picture by a combination of separate details — for instance, they had been commissioned to produce a group picture of people who, for one reason or another, could not be photographed together but only singly. They copied or pasted together single pictures in front of a common, mostly scenic, background and no one was to notice that the group had been pieced together. That then was the first photomontage.

The Dadaists enlarged the meaning of photomontage. Partly in order to astonish, partly to give a demonstration, partly to create optical poems, they pasted together pieces of different photographs. These parts of pictures, pieced together, often achieved a rather enigmatic meaning that was difficult to unravel, and yet had a provocative effect. These pictures were far from pretending to be real; they showed brutally the process, the dissection of single photos, the crude cut made by scissors. These 'photomontages' were true sisters to Futurist, brutalist music which, composed of scraps of noise, in its gathering together of many elements sought to convey the exciting experience of the awakening of a metropolis and similar things.

In comparison with this, photo-sculpture is a sort of organized apparition. Its pictures have a well-defined meaning and central idea; and though they often consist of different optical and intellectual superimpositions and interlockings it is possible to have a clear view of the total situation. In this they correspond approximately to the construction of a fugue or the arrangement of an orchestra, both of which, though built up from more or less numerous superimpositions, produce in their totality a clear meaning. The effect of photo-sculptures is based on the mutual penetration and fusion of connections which in real life are not always visible, on a comprehension by means of a picture of the simultaneity of events.

Until the Futurists entered the scene, the concept of simultaneity had existed in the brain, intellectually, but it had not been experienced consciously by the senses. The Futurists touched on this problem not only in their music but also in their pictures: 'the noise of the street penetrates the house' or 'memory of the night of the ball' etc. But the construction of Futurist pictures was as yet not very dynamic in comparison with photomontages. Against this, Dadaist photomontage, in its unruliness, in its big leaps, was mostly too individualistic to be understood quickly. It wanted too much: it wanted to achieve on a plane, in the static stage, a kinetic motion which was reversed for film. It set itself a task that was over-ambitious; so vision failed.

The difference between photomontage and photo-sculpture is already clear from their techniques. Like photomontage, photo-sculpture is made up from different photographs that are pasted together, retouched, and compressed in one plane. But photo-sculpture tries to remain moderate in its presentation of simultaneity. It is clear, arranged lucidly and uses photographic elements in a concentrated way, having divested itself of all disturbing accessories. It shows situations in a state of compression which can be unwound very quickly by the process of association.

This economical method makes understanding easier and often reveals all of a sudden an otherwise hidden meaning.

One has confidence in the objectivity of photography of a type which does not seem to permit the subjective interpretation of an event. As a result of this confidence and by the combination of photographic elements with lines and other supplements, one obtains unexpected tensions which reach far beyond the significance of the single parts. It would be hardly possible to achieve a similar effect by using simple drawing or painting to convey forms. For it is just this integration of photographically presented elements of events, the simple, as well as the complicated superimpositions, which produce a curious unity moving on optically prescribed paths, as it were on rails of ideas. This unity can have various effects, amusing, moving, despairing, satirical, visionary, revolutionary etc.

Photo-sculpture is often the expression of an intellectually hardly comprehensible variety of combinations. It is frequently a very bitter joke, often blasphemous. Often it shows the evil side of man; often, too, it rebels against insufficiency: it is clownish and witty, tragic and serious.

Photo-sculpture is based on visual and mental gymnastics presented in more concentrated form than that which befalls a city-dweller on his daily rounds.

Example: one rides in a tram, looks out through a window. There is a car behind. The windows of this car are also transparent. Through them one sees a shop which in its turn has transparent windows. In the shop there are people, buyers and salesmen. Somebody else opens the door. People pass by the shop. The traffic policeman stops a bicyclist. All this one grasps in a single moment because the window panes are transparent and everything that happens is seen by looking in the same direction.

A similar process occurs in photo-sculpture — on another level — not as a summing up but as a synthesis: here the superimpositions and penetrations are formed by intellectual associations and the sense of vision.

In this way photographic methods can be used to produce experiences and intellectual associations which cannot be achieved to the same degree by other means. The visual and the intellectual become accessible in a moment, they have to become accessible in a moment if the effect is to be achieved. That is why a balance in the composition of intellectual and optical factors is here especially important. However, the construction of the photo-sculpture picture is not a composition in the earlier sense, it does not aim at a formal harmony but is rather a composition pointing to a given end, that of the presentation of ideas.

If we can assume a knowledge of the present, of different cultures, political events, current problems etc., the speed with which optical impressions and their associations are received can be extraordinarily fast. That is why a photo-sculpture sheet cannot be understood by an Eskimo. On the other hand a non-objective picture is accessible to everyone as it rests in biological laws of purely optical experiences which function in all people.

It is possible that city-dwellers, too, have difficulties with photo-sculptures at first. But people who have always to show presence of mind, e.g. those who often have to drive a car in difficult situations, will have much quicker reactions than those who are not accustomed to a keen observation of life around them and to paying attention to the first sign of a threatening danger.

It is therefore sensible to start a demonstration with simple superimpositions and to facilitate understanding by the use of striking, comprehensive titles.

Photo-sculptures can be used in different ways.

One of many possibilities: the scenic intensification of whole sequences in theatre and film: plays and filmscripts can be condensed into a single picture.

Another kind of use: the illustration of a concept or a feeling.

As illustration for propaganda, advertisements, posters.

As topical satire, etc.

The joke of the future will probably not be illustrated graphically but by means of photo-sculptures. Similarly, the cinema posters of the future will be produced by photographic and photo-sculptural means which, unquestionably, correspond better to the nature of film than do today's posters which are done by drawing and poetically coloured to illustrate scenes in the film.

Only recently have people started to explore this new field. But one will soon notice that every material, however difficult it may appear, will after a little while prove easier to handle.

[Printed in *Bauhaus* No. 1, 1928, pp. 2ff.]

L. Moholy-Nagy:
Painting and Photography

Among the obscure concepts in the fine arts are painting and photography.

Nowadays painting and photography are frequently played off, one against the other. It is claimed that of the two only painting is an expression of inner emotion and that photography is nothing but a mechanical reproduction of reality, and must not be allowed a claim to be counted among the arts.

However, a thorough investigation shows that both fields deal with problems of optical manipulation. From the present-day point of view, optical manipulation is one of the unconscious, unintended means of education which we use in order to prepare a form of consciousness that is suitable for a future society. We do not mean here, in the first instance, the so-called propaganda art which is recognized as important and constantly in demand by active politicians. Here the point is, above all, to activate by means of the optical organ forces hidden in the unconscious. True, political activists reject values obtained in this manner as 'aesthetic', but that is only because these people are so pre-occupied with the most burning problems of the day that they fight shy of any supposed complications. That such an attitude on the part of 'professional revolutionaries' deeply offends many artists, and can shake their solidarity with political actions is something we have to ascribe to the artists' own lack of clarity with regard to their task within society as a whole.

We live in a revolutionary period. The dialectic process of development compels us, in the distorting mirror of more forceful reactionary trends that grow day by day, to examine our concepts and to clarify our work.

Since the inception of industrial socialism, we know that social relations are essentially determined by economic relations and our actions are determined by social relations.

We know now that this is also the essence of all artistic action and that the problem (the content of consciousness) in the work of artistic manipulation is not different from that in other creative disciplines.

Our crucial problem is that capitalism brought us to a stage of economics and racial development where life has become intolerable from the point of view of a healthy and fulfilling occupation.

The class struggle is a means, a very effective political means, for the removal of these grievances, for the improvement of the organic conditions of life. But there exist also other means, less conscious and purposeful, but which have the aim of giving man an idea of what is necessary for him for a later reconstruction of life after the present total or at least partial shattering of these energies.

Art is this unconscious preparation, the subconscious education of man.

[Introduction to a lecture, given in Cologne in December 1931, printed in *a bis z* ('a to z, the organ of the group of progressive artists'), 23, Cologne, April 1932, 3rd series, p. 89]

Documentary sources concerning the development of the photogram

A letter from Moholy to Walter Gropius, 16 December 1935

'[p. 9] . . . this is how the matter stands: I had long believed that I had discovered the procedure for producing photograms. In July 1922, in *De Stijl*, I published an article on "production – reproduction" in which I proposed the production of photograms as creative photography, as well as the production of acoustic fixations (drawing on gramophone disks). Later on I extended this idea to synthetic sound film writing (in my book *Painting, Photography, Film*).

[added in the margin:] I acted entirely in good faith regarding my discovery and I am certain that van Doesburg would never have published the article as a discovery if he had heard of Man Ray's photograms. Besides, I should like to see anyone who, like me, had no previous knowledge of photographic technique, would then have written up the procedure after the reproduction of a strange photogram. I made my first photograms on daylight sensitive paper [*sic*!] as I had not taken any photographs at all until then (except for an attempt to photograph 2 superimposed photos as a portrait of my friend Carl Koch).[1] From that point in time I began seriously to analyse photographic problems in general.

In the autumn of 1922 Harold Loeb and Matthew Josephson, the editors of the American periodical *Broom*, came to visit me to ask for the right to publish my photograms [p. 10] and they told me that an American photographer, Man Ray, of whom I had not heard until then, was also producing photograms. Mine were "more interesting", however. (The above is merely to outline the situation.) I presented them both with an article about "light as a creative element of manipulation" and in the March 1923 issue of *Broom* they published four of my photograms and four by Man Ray, together with my article . . .'

In the same letter [p. 11] Moholy stresses: 'I certainly invented the name "photogram". In my book (vol. 8 [of the Bauhaus series]) I gave this kind of photography this name (by analogy with the word "telegram"), but even this word is old. Around 1860 people used it for photographic prints. However, I learnt this also only much later when I knew more about these matters – also historically. My entire work until then had been rather more intuitive and cavalier than scientifically well founded.'

[Bauhaus-Archiv, Berlin, Gropius Estate 9/3/46–80]

Lucia Moholy: *Marginalien zu Moholy-Nagy/Moholy-Nagy, Marginal Notes* (bilingual edition)

Lucia Moholy stresses that only after a 'stroll in the Rhön mountains' did Moholy and she together turn to photography; that she had herself first been instructed by a photographer in Weimar in 1923 and built a simple darkroom. According to this statement, all the pictures on sensitized paper are of an earlier date. Allegedly, Moholy himself never mastered photographic procedures in a laboratory. Hence, to produce photograms in the darkroom both Lucia and László Moholy were always needed. The 'double portrait', Laci and Lucia, is a little monument to their collaboration. It is obvious that Lucia Moholy (who, later on, gave magnificent proof of her talent as a photographer) also contributed, beyond her technical expertise, to the development of the creative possibilities. Moholy's later statement (in *Vision in Motion*, p. 72) suggesting that work with photograms had begun in 1920 is refuted by all the known sources.

'. . . the beginning of the idea dated back to the pre-Bauhaus period. I clearly remember how it came about. During a stroll in the Rhön mountains in the summer of 1922 we discussed the problem arising from the antithesis Production versus Reproduction. This gradually led us to implement our conclusions by making photograms, independently of any ideas formulated by Schad, Man Ray and Lissitzky (or others for that matter) . . . The deliberations which formed the basis of our activities were published in *De Stijl* 7/1922 and reprinted in other magazines. A section was devoted to the subject in

---

1 Apropos Carl Koch, Moholy wrote in 1925: 'The manuscript sketch "Dynamic of the Metropolis" was written in 1921–22. I hoped to carry it out together with my friend Carl Koch who gave me many ideas for this piece of work.' (see *Painting, Photography, Film*, p. 122).

Malerei Photographie Film, in 1925 ...' (cf. Painting Photography Film, p. 32).
[Lucia Moholy, Moholy-Nagy, Marginal Notes, Krefeld 1972, p. 59]

A letter from Lissitzky to Sophie Küppers, Moscow, 15 September 1925

'1. 1921–2. When I went to Berlin and met Hausmann in Moholy's studio, it was decided to publish a periodical. I made out its programme dealing with *productive*, not reproductive, achievements. At that time Moholy still had no *special subject.* I drew his attention to *photography.* He was just preparing his first exhibition for *Der Sturm.* Neither Hausmann nor I took him seriously. At our meeting Hausmann showed us some cuttings from American periodicals about optophonetics. There were two abstract photos among them, to which I drew Moholy's attention. I am not sure whether they were by Man Ray, because his name was not yet known to any of us.

2. Spring 1922. Dada Conference in Weimar. Tzara tells us about "Les Champs délicieux". Subsequently displayed a few pages in Berlin and Moholy was extremely interested in their style of production and got all possible information out of Tzara.

3. In the meantime, in 1922–3, he had got to know Loeb and acquired further knowledge. He went to these people and saw the photos by Man Ray, because they were preparing an issue. Moholy did a series of "abstract photos"!

4. When the issue was being put together, Moholy suppressed the things by Man Ray (after all he was far away . . . in Paris), and he soon got rid of Loeb-Josephson. From Man Ray's photos he selected those which did not too strongly resemble his, then he spiked the article by Man Ray, and himself cooked up an intellectual hotchpotch of all our slogans. And thus he feigned an achievement. Losovik, who was the translator for *Broom* and also translated Moholy's writings, told me all this. Neither Loeb nor Josephson, Losovik or I thought any more about it: for it is in fact the same thing as saying that Richter discovered the abstract film.

5. In *Das Kunstblatt* (current year of issue, first appearing here) Harold Loeb saw an article "Photo-graphie ohne Apparat" with your illustrations, where the subject is very lucidly dealt with.

So you have the witnesses – Hausmann, Tzara, Losovik, Loeb, Lissitzky – but they are not required at all. One should look at the work itself. Moholy wanted to demonstrate to us that Man Ray is a Dadaist: objects, no representation of light, etc. But Moholy created an abstract light-pattern. The *artistic merit* of the discovery is something completely created by Man Ray. He reaches the point of perversity in his complete abstraction of light. The underlying theme is both eccentric and American. There you have something of merit, and it has character too, even in its weaknesses, because it is alive.

What has Moholy contributed to it? Light? It has been left in the air. Painting? Moholy doesn't know the first thing about that. Theme? Where is that to be found? In order to concentrate you've got to have a focal point. Character? That's the mask they always hide behind. It's idiotic of me to be taking this Moholy business so seriously but this plagiarism is already getting to be too bare-faced.'
[S. Lissitzky-Küppers, *El Lissitzky: Life. Letters. Text*, pp. 66f.]

Lissitzky refers perhaps to discussions about Moholy's discovery of the photogram on the occasion of the appearance in 1925 of his book *Malerei Photographie Film*, about which Sophie Küppers had told him.

Lissitzky does *not* mention that he, too, had produced photograms before Moholy. This does not render any more plausible the date '1920', given without stating a source, for two photograms of Lissitzky's which have recently been shown in numerous exhibitions (cf., for example, 'Die 20er Jahre in Osteuropa', Galerie Gmurzinska, Cologne, June–Sept. 1975, nos. 63, 64). However, the suggestion that Lissitzky had brought with him the concept of 'productive art' from the Soviet Union is important. Lissitzky's, as also later on Kemény's, undisguised hostility towards Moholy the 'plagiarist' is probably directed especially against Moholy's 'betrayal' of the socialist and Constructivist ideal by joining the Bauhaus which was described as bourgeois. As a matter of fact the removal of Itten and the appointment of Moholy in his place were the most important actions by which, from 1923 onwards, Gropius sought to rid the Bauhaus of the odium of romantic and idealist backwardness.

Biography of Moholy-Nagy

1895 Born 20 July in Bácbarsòd (Southern Hungary). His father (a farm manager) left his family early on and emigrated to the U.S.A. László, with his mother and brother, was received into the house of his uncle (a lawyer). The name 'Moholy' refers to the place of origin of the family, Mohol, and was only later on added by László to the family name 'Nagy'.

1913 Accepted as student of law by the University of Budapest.

1914 War service as artillery officer in the Austro-Hungarian army.

1915 After suffering concussion, stay in a hospital during which he produced his first crayon drawings and watercolours.

1917 Severely wounded. During convalescence in Odessa and Szeged, does aquarelles and drawings. Founds with friends a short-lived literary periodical, *Jelenkor*, to which he contributes poems, short stories and book reviews.

1918 Resumes the study of law which, however, he does not complete – despite passing some examinations.

1919 Works in Szeged as an artist and exhibits some of his works. Seeks contacts with the Communist Party but gets no encouragement from Béla Kun, the Chairman of the Council of Commissars. After the defeat of the Hungarian Soviet Republic, LM-N emigrates to Vienna, where he joins the circle of other Hungarian refugees around the 'activist' periodical *Ma*, whose leader is Lajos Kassák. Close contacts with the *Ma*-artists Béla Uitz and Nemes Lamperth had already existed since 1918.

1920 At beginning of the year moves to Berlin. Contacts with *Der Sturm* and the Dadaists, Schwitters, Höch and Hausmann. Gets to know Lucia Schultz who had studied the history of art and philosophy in Prague; they are married in 1921.

1921 Becomes the Berlin correspondent for the periodical *Ma* which is published in Vienna. Together with R. Hausmann, H. Arp and I. Puni, he publishes the *Manifesto on Elemental Art*. At the end of the year he meets El Lissitzky.

1922 First one-man show, in the gallery 'Der Sturm'. As representative of *Ma* group takes part in the Congress of Progressive Artists in Düsseldorf, similarly in the Congress of Constructivists and Dadaists in Weimar. Publishes the article 'Production – Reproduction' and, with Alfred Kemény, the manifesto 'Dynamisch-Konstruktives Kräftesystem' (dynamic-constructive system of forces). Edits, together with L. Kassák, the *Buch neuer Kunstler* (Book of New Artists). Produces, in collaboration with his wife Lucia, his first camera-less pictures – photograms.

1923 In spring he becomes a teacher at the Bauhaus in Weimar, first as director of the metal workshop, later – as successor to Johannes Itten – as director of the foundation course. Lucia Moholy studies photography. At the Bauhaus, Schwerdtferger and Hirschfeld-Mack try out their 'Reflectory Light Displays'. Moholy publishes his article 'light – a medium of plastic expression' in the American periodical *Broom*.

1924–25 Occupies himself, together with Oskar Schlemmer and Farkas Molnar with theatre, dance and ballet. Edits, together with Walter Gropius, the first volumes in the series of 'Bauhaus Books' (among them vol. 8, his own *Painting Photography Film*). 1925 journey with Giedion and his wife to Paris and Belle-Ile-en-Mer. Intense activity with camera photography.

1925–26 Because of political attacks from the Right, the Bauhaus is dissolved in Weimar and moves to Dessau. Gropius is the architect of the Dessau buildings. The masters move into the new masters' houses. 1926, journey with Schlemmer and his family to Ascona.

1927 Participates with J. J. P. Oud and Willem Pijper in the foundation of the periodical *10* (Amsterdam) and edits the photographic section.

1928 Leaves the Bauhaus, together with Gropius and

Herbert Bayer, and moves first to Berlin. Prepares the book *Von Material zu Architektur* (English edition [1947]: *The New Vision. From Material to Architecture*), and says in his preface: 'manuscript and corrections of the book have been worked on by my wife, Lucia Moholy, who clarified and enriched the book in many ways'.

1929 Separation from Lucia Moholy sees the end of their common work on photography. Moholy expands his activities to include exhibition design and stage design (Berlin State Opera House and Piscator theatre) as well as commercial graphic design, title pages of the periodical *die neue linie.* Journey to Marseilles; the film *Marseille vieux port.* Prepares important parts of the Deutsche Werkbund exhibition 'Film und Foto' in Stuttgart, in which 97 photographic works of his own are shown. Public break-through on a broad front of the 'new photography'. Moholy gives numerous lectures.

1930 Participation in the exhibition of the Deutsche Werkbund in Paris where he exhibits his 'Licht-requisit für eine elektrische Bühne' (light requisite for an electric stage), following which he produces his abstract film *Lichtspiel Schwarz-Weiss-Grau* (Light Display, Black and White and Grey). Travels in Scandinavia. Meets Mrs Sibylle Pietzsch, later to become his second wife.

1933 Participation in the international architectural congress, C.I.A.M., in Greece.

1934 Emigration to Amsterdam where he has to take on more and more commercial work (photo and colour experiments for a printing firm, design of a textile exhibition).

1935 With the support of Herbert Read, moves to London where Walter Gropius had settled shortly before. In a group of artists, 'The Circle', meets, among others, Henry Moore and Barbara Hepworth. Designs the stand for Courtauld's at the Industrial Fair. Becomes artistic adviser to Simpson's of Piccadilly (window display), and to Royal Airlines and London Transport (graphic design). Receives a commission to illustrate three books with photographs: *Street Markets of London*, *Eton Portrait* and *An Oxford University Chest.*

1936 Designs utopian light decorations for Alexander Korda's film 'The Shape of Things to Come' (after H. G. Wells) which are, however, not accepted by the producer.

1937 At the instigation of Walter Gropius, who had gone to U.S.A. at the beginning of the year, Moholy applies successfully for the position of director of a design school in Chicago which was to be opened by the 'Association of Arts and Industry'. Names it the New Bauhaus — American School of Design. Because of personal and financial difficulties the school has to close down only one year later. Contract as designer and graphic artist on advertisements for the export firm Spiegel Inc.

1939 Moholy, together with the staff of the New Bauhaus (among others G. Kepes, H. Bredendieck, H. H. Smith, C. Eckart, Ch. Morris) founded a school of their own, the 'School of Design'. The enterprise is financially supported by Walter Paepcke, the President of the Container Corporation of America. Further grants from Rockefeller Foundation and Carnegie Corporation. Contracts as designer with Parker Pen Co., the Baltimore and Ohio Railroad, and others.

1940–44 Development of the School of Design. Extensive artistic and scientific teaching programme comprising, among other subjects, economics, psychology, information theory and biology.

1944 The School becomes The Institute of Design with a strongly organized administrative Council whose members are leading industrialists. At the end of Moholy's life the Institute of Design has 680 students.

1946 Moholy dies in Chicago of leukaemia on 24 November. His book *Vision in Motion* appears posthumously in 1947.

Select Bibliography

(a) Works by Moholy-Nagy

Books

1 *Buch neuer Künstler* (with Lajos Kassák), Vienna 1922.
2 *Die Bühne am Bauhaus* (with Oskar Schlemmer and Farkas Molnár), Bauhaus Book no. 4, Munich 1925.
3 *Malerei Photographie Film*, Bauhaus Book no. 8, Munich 1925; 2nd expanded ed., *Malerei Fotografie Film*, Munich 1927. English trans. by Janet Seligman, *Painting Photography Film*, London and Cambridge, Mass. 1969, based on the 1927 edition.
4 *Von Material zu Architektur*, Bauhaus Book no. 14, Munich 1929; facsimile ed. in the series 'Neue Bauhausbücher', Mainz 1968. English trans. by Daphne M. Hoffmann, *The New Vision: from Material to Architecture*, New York n.d. (1930); 4th ed., New York 1947, expanded to include an autobiographical section 'Abstract of an Artist'.
5 *Vision in Motion*, Chicago 1947.

Manifestos, articles and essays
(listed chronologically)
Various articles by and about Moholy-Nagy appeared in a special number of Telehor 1/2, Brno 1936; *see individual entries below.*

1 'Aufruf zur elementaren Kunst – an die Künstler der Welt!' (with Raoul Hausmann, Hans Arp and Ivan Puni), in *De Stijl* V, no. 4 (October 1921); cf. Appendix, p. 46.
2 'Produktion – Reproduktion', in *De Stijl* V, no. 7 (July 1922); cf. Appendix, p. 46.
3 'Dynamisch-Konstruktives Kräftesystem' (manifesto on Kinetic Sculpture, with Alfred Kemény), in *Der Sturm* 12, Berlin 1922; English trans. in *Vision in Motion*, Chicago 1947, p. 238, and R. Kostelanetz (ed.), *Moholy-Nagy*, New York 1970 and London 1971, p. 29.
4 'Vita az új tartalom és az új forma problémájárol' ('problems of new content and new form'), in *Akasztott Ember*, Vienna, December 1922.
5 'Die neue Typographie', in *Staatliches Bauhaus Weimar 1919–23*, Munich-Weimar 1923; English trans. in R. Kostelanetz (ed.), op. cit., pp. 75f.
6 'Light – a Medium of Plastic Expression', in *Broom* IV, New York–Berlin, March 1923; reprinted in N. Lyons (ed.), *Photographers on Photography*, Englewood Cliffs, N.J.; cf. also R. Kostelanetz (ed.), op. cit., pp. 117f.
7 'Fotoplastische Reklame', in *Offset, Buch und Werbekunst* 7, Leipzig 1926.
8 'geradlinigkeit des geistes – umwege der technik', in *Bauhaus* I, no. 1, Dessau 1926; English trans. in R. Kostelanetz (ed.), op. cit., pp. 187f.
9 'Ismus oder Kunst', in *Vivos Voco* V, 8/9, Leipzig, September 1926; English trans. by Sibyl Moholy-Nagy in R. Kostelanetz (ed.), op. cit., pp. 34ff.
10 'Die beispiellose Fotografie', in *i 10 Internationale Revue*, vol. 1, no. 3, Amsterdam 1927; also in *Das deutsche Lichtbild*, 1927, pp. x–xi.
11 'eine programmandeutung für fotografische arbeit', in *Führer VDAV* (Verband Deutscher Amateurphotographenvereine), Berlin 1927, pp. 19–23.
12 'Die Photographie in der Reklame', in *Photographische Korrespondenz* LXIII, September 1927.
13 'Der sprechende Film', in *i 10 Internationale Revue*, vol. 1, nos. 17/18, Amsterdam 1928.
14 'fotografie ist lichtgestaltung', in *Bauhaus* II, no. 1, pp. 2ff., Dessau 1928; also, with slight alterations, under the title 'Photographie ist Lichtgestaltung', in *Photographische Korrespondenz*, 1 May 1928.
15 'Neue Wege in der Photographie', in *Photographische Rundschau*, 1928, pp. 33–6.
16 'Experimentale Fotografie', in *Das neue Frankfurt* III, no. 3, 1929.
17 'Filmkroniek', in *i 10 Internationale Revue*, vol. 1, no. 19, Amsterdam 1929.
18 'Fotogramm und Grenzgebiete', in *Die Form* IV, Berlin 1929.
19 'La photographie ce qu'elle était, ce qu'elle devra être', in *Cahiers d'Art* IV, no. 1, Paris 1929.
20 'The future of the photographic Process', in *Transition*, Paris, 15 February 1929.
21 'Wohin geht die photographische Entwicklung?', in *Agfa-Photoblätter*, 1931–2, pp. 267–72.
22 'Einleitung zum Vortrag "malerei und fotografie", Köln Dezember 1931', in *a bis z* 3/23, Cologne, April 1932, p. 89. Cf. Appendix, p. 50.

23 'Probleme des neuen Films' (written in 1928, and delivered as a lecture at the tenth 'Bildwoche' in Dresden), printed in *Die Form* 5, Berlin 1932. Published as 'Problèmes du nouveau film' in *Cahiers d'Art* VII, nos. 6/7, Paris 1932. See also *New Cinema* 1, London 1934; *Telehor*, Brno 1936; and R. Kostelanetz (ed.), op. cit., pp. 131ff.

24 'An Open Letter' in *Sight and Sound* III (1934), no. 10; reprinted in *Vision in Motion*, pp. 272ff.

25 'How photography revolutionises vision', in *The Listener*, London, 8 November 1933; German version (1932) under the title 'fotografie, die objektive sehform unserer zeit', published in *Telehor*, Brno 1936.

26 'Offener Brief an die Filmindustrie und an Alle, die Interesse an der Entwicklung des guten Films haben', in *Ekran* 1, no. 1, Brno, 15 November 1934.

27 Letter to F. Kalivoda, June 1934, printed in *Telehor*, 1936; English translation in R. Kostelanetz (ed.), op. cit., pp. 37ff.

28 Supplement to 'probleme des neuen films' (no. 23, above), written in London in 1935; printed in *Telehor*, 1936. Cf. R. Kostelanetz (ed.), op. cit., pp. 139ff.

29 'Subject without Art' (reply to R. H. Wilenski), in *Modern Photography, The Studio* XII, London, 4 November 1936; cf. R. Kostelanetz (ed.), op. cit., pp. 42f.

30 'Vom Pigment zum Licht', in *Telehor*, 1936; English translation ('From Pigment to Light') in R. Kostelanetz (ed.), op. cit., pp. 30ff.

31 'Light Architecture', in *Industrial Arts* I, no. 1 (Spring), London 1936; cf. R. Kostelanetz (ed.), op. cit., pp. 155ff.

32 'Photography in a Flash', in *Industrial Arts* I, no. 4 (Winter), London 1936; cf. R. Kostelanetz (ed.) op. cit., pp. 54ff.

33 'Light Painting', in J. L. Martin, Ben Nicholson and Naum Gabo, *Circle: International Survey of Constructive Art*, London 1937.

34 'Richtlijnen vor een onbelemmerde kleurenfotografie', in *Prisma der Kunsten*, Zeist 1937.

35 'Paths to the unleashed Colour Camera, in *The Penrose Annual* XXXIX, London 1937; cf. R. Kostelanetz (ed.), op. cit., pp. 66ff.

36 'Light: A New Medium of Expression', in *Architectural Forum* LXX, Chicago, May 1939; cf. R. Kostelanetz (ed.), op. cit., pp. 151ff.

37 'Painting with Light – A New Medium of Expression', in *The Penrose Annual* XL, London 1939.

38 'About the Elements of Motion Picture', in *Design*, Columbus, Ohio, October 1942.

39 'Photography', in *A Pageant of Photography*, San Francisco, 1940.

40 'Space-Time and the Photographer', in *American Annual of Photography 1943*, LVII, Boston, Mass., 1942; cf. R. Kostelanetz (ed.), op. cit., pp. 57ff.

41 'Surrealism and the Photographer', in *The Complete Photographer* 52, 1943.

42 'Photography in the Study of Design', in *American Annual of Photography 1945*, LIX, Boston, Mass., 1944.

43 'The Coming World of Photography', in *Popular Photography* XIV, no. 2, New York 1944.

44 'On Art and the Photograph', in *The Technology Review* XLVII, no. 8, Cambridge, Mass., June 1945.

45 'Photography', in Dagobert D. Runes and Harry G. Schickel, *Encyclopedia of the Arts*, New York 1946.

Photographic works

1 *Moholy-Nagy 60 Fotos*, edited and with an introduction ('Moholy-Nagy und die neue Fotografie') by Franz Roh, Berlin 1930; English trans. of introduction in R. Kostelanetz (ed.), op. cit., pp. 49f.

2 *The Street Markets of London*, with text by Mary Benedetta, London 1936.

3 *Eton Portrait*, with text by Bernard Ferguson, London 1937.

4 *An Oxford University Chest*, with text by John Betjeman, London 1939.

Films

1 *Berliner Stilleben*, 1926.

2 *Marseille Vieux Port*, 1929.

3 *Lichtspiel Schwarz-Weiss-Grau*, 1930. See scenario ('light display, black and white and grey') in *Vision in Motion* (§ Books: 5), p. 288; cf. also R. Kostelanetz (ed.), op. cit. pp. 148ff.

4 *Tönendes ABC*, 1932.

5 *Zigeuner*, 1932.

6 *Architektenkongreß Athen*, 1933.

7 *Life of a Lobster*, 1935.

8 *The New Architecture at the London Zoo*, 1936.

Film scenarios

1 *Dynamik der Großstadt*, 1921/2. Reproduced with illustrations as 'Dynamic of the Metropolis', in *Painting Photography Film* (§ Books: 3); cf. also R. Kostelanetz (ed.), op. cit., pp. 118ff.

2 *Huhn bleibt Huhn*, in *Telehor* 1/2, 1936. English translation in Myfanwy Evans (ed.), *The Painter's Object*, London 1937, pp. 136ff.; see also *Vision in Motion* (§ Books: 5), pp. 285ff., and R. Kostelanetz (ed.), op. cit., pp. 124ff.

(b) Works on Moholy-Nagy (listed alphabetically by author)

Various articles by and about Moholy-Nagy, including an Introduction by Sigfried Giedion and a Postscript by F. Kalivoda, appeared in a special number of Telehor *1/2, Brno 1936; cf.* § *Manifestos etc., above.*

Beke, László, 'László Moholy-Nagy, the Light-Artist', in *Interpressgrafik* 1977/1, Budapest.

Brendel, János, 'László Moholy-Nagy, Twórczósc artistry do 1923 Roku', in *Studia Muzealne* IX, Poznan 1971, pp. 70–87.

Bruns, Renée, 'L. Moholy-Nagy; a portfolio of images never before published by a master who influenced Modern Design', in *Popular Photography* LXXV, no. 2, August 1974.

Engelbrecht, Lloyd C., 'László Moholy-Nagy. Perfecting the Eye by Means of Photography', in Rice and Steadman (ed.), *Photographs of Moholy-Nagy . . .*, 1975 – see below;

——, 'Moholy in Chicago', in *László Moholy-Nagy*, published by Verlag Gerd Hatje, Stuttgart 1974 – see Hatje, below.

Erfurth, Hugo, 'Moholy-Nagy', in *Qualität* (Zeitung für Ware und Werbung) IX, nos. 1–2, Dessau 1931.

Fawkes, Caroline, 'Photography and Moholy-Nagy's Do-it-yourself Aesthetic', in *Studio International* CXC, July–August 1975;

——, 'From the Bauhaus: L. Moholy-Nagy', in *Camera* XLVI, April 1967.

Grobleben, Paul, 'Moholy-Nagy. Photographie der Gegenwart und wir!', in *Photofreund* 24, 1929.

Hatje, Gerd (publisher), in collaboration with Hannah Weitemeier, Wulf Herzogenrath, Tilman Osterwald and Lloyd C. Engelbrecht, *László Moholy-Nagy*, Stuttgart 1974; French edition, Centre National d'Art et de Culture Georges Pompidou, Paris 1976.

Kallai, Ernst (Ernö), 'Ladislaus Moholy-Nagy', in *Jahrbuch der jungen Kunst*, vol. 5, Leipzig 1924.

Kepes, György, 'László Moholy-Nagy: the Bauhaus Tradition', in *Print* XXIII, no. 1, New York, Jan.–Feb. 1969.

Koppe, Richard, 'László Moholy-Nagy and his visions', in *Art International* XIII, no. 10, Christmas 1969.

Kostelanetz, Richard (ed.), *Moholy-Nagy*, New York 1970, and London 1971; includes several articles written by Moholy (see § Manifestos etc., above).

Kovacs, Istvan, 'Totality through light. The work of László Moholy-Nagy', in *Form*, no. 6, Cambridge, 6 December 1967.

Kuh, Katherine, 'Moholy-Nagy in Chicago', in *L. Moholy-Nagy*, The Art Institute of Chicago, 1947.

Mátyàs, Peter (= E. Kallai), *Horizont 2*, Vienna 1921;

——, 'Moholy-Nagy', in *Ma* 12, Vienna 1921.

Moholy, Lucia, *Marginalien zu Moholy-Nagy – Moholy-Nagy, Marginal Notes* (bilingual edition), Krefeld 1972.

Moholy-Nagy, Sibyl, 'Documented Seeing', in *Art and Photography*, Chicago 1949;

——, *Moholy-Nagy. Experiment in Totality*, New York 1950; 2nd ed., Cambridge, Mass., and London 1969; German trans., *László Moholy-Nagy, ein Total-experiment*, published as no. 13 of the series 'Neue Bauhausbücher', Mainz-Berlin 1972.

Newhall, Beaumont, 'The Photography of Moholy-Nagy', in *The Kenyon Review* III/4 (Summer 1941), Gambier, Ohio.

Passuth, Krisztina, 'Début of László Moholy-Nagy', in *Acta Historiae Artium Academiae Scientiarium Hungaricae* XIX, 1973, pp. 125–42;

——, *Magyar muvészek az európai avantgarde – ban 1919–1925*, Budapest 1974.

Péter, László, 'The young Years of Moholy-Nagy', in *The New Hungarian Quarterly* XIII/46 (Summer 1972), pp. 62–72.

Read, Herbert, 'A New Humanism', in *The Architectural Review* LXXVIII, London, October 1935; cf. R. Kostelanetz (ed.), op. cit., pp. 170ff.

Reichardt, Jasia, 'Moholy-Nagy and Light Art as an Art of the Future', in *Studio International*, London, November 1967.

Rice, Leland D., and David W. Steadman (ed.), *Photographs of Moholy-Nagy from the Collection of William Larson*, The Galleries of Claremont Colleges, Pomona College, Scripps College, Claremont, Cal., 1975: Introduction by Rice.

Roh, Franz, Introduction: 'Moholy-Nagy und die neue Fotografie', in F. Roh (ed.), *Moholy-Nagy 60 Fotos*, Berlin 1930.

Rondolino, Giovanni, *László Moholy-Nagy, Pittura, Fotografia, Film* (with Preface by Giulio Carlo Argan), Turin 1975.

Smith, Henry Holmes, 'Across the Atlantic and out of the Woods. Moholy-Nagy's Contribution to Photography in the United States', in Rice and Steadman (ed.), op. cit.

Starke, H., 'Der Sinn der modernen Photographie. Ein Vortrag von Professor Moholy-Nagy', in 'Photospiegel' (supplement to *Berliner Tageblatt*, no. 44), 1929.

Steadman, David W. – see Rice and Steadman, above.

Steckel-Weitemeier, Hannah, 'László Moholy-Nagy 1895 bis 1946, Entwurf seiner Wahrnehmungslehre', thesis (1974) submitted to the Freie Universität, West Berlin.

Travis, David, 'László Moholy-Nagy', in the catalogue *Photographs from the Julien Levy Collection*, The Art Institute of Chicago, 11 December 1976–20 February 1977.

Warstadt, Willy, 'Die "entfesselte Kamera" und die "produktive Photographie". Zu den Ideen Professor Moholy-Nagys', in *Deutscher Kamera-Almanach*, 1929.

Weitemeier, Hannah, 'Vision in Motion', in *Moholy-Nagy*, Stedelijk van Abbe Museum, Eindhoven 1967; and *Avant-garde Osteuropa 1910–30*, West Berlin 1967;

——, *Licht-Visionen. Ein Experiment von Moholy-Nagy*, Bauhaus Archiv, West Berlin 1972.

(c) General works on Moholy-Nagy's art and photography

Ades, Dawn, *Photomontage*, London and New York 1976.

Banham, Reyner, *Theory and Design in the First Machine Age*, London and New York 1960 (see especially pp. 312–19).

Beiler, Berthold, *Die Gewalt des Augenblicks. Gedanken zur Ästhetik der Fotografie*, 2nd ed., Leipzig 1969.

Coke, Van Deren, *The Painter and the Photographer*, University of New Mexico Press, Albuquerque 1964.

Egbert, Donald D., *Social Radicalism and the Arts. Western Europe*, New York 1970.

Franciscono, Marcel, *Walter Gropius and the Creation of the Bauhaus in Weimar*, Urbana, Ill., 1971.

Gropius, Walter, with Herbert Bayer and Ise Gropius, *Bauhaus 1919–28*, New York 1938.

Grote, Ludwig, *Die Maler am Bauhaus*, Munich 1950.

Kahmen, Volker, *Fotografie als Kunst*, Tübingen 1973.

Lissitzky-Küppers, Sophie, *El Lissitzky: Life. Letters. Texts,* London and Greenwich, Conn., 1968 (trans. from the German; see note 19).

Moholy, Lucia, 'Das Bauhaus-Bild', in *Werk–Schweizer Monatsschrift für Architektur, Kunst, Kunsthistorische Gewerbe* LV, June 1968.

Newhall, Beaumont, *The History of Photography from 1839 to the present day*, 2nd ed., New York 1964.

Rose, Barbara, 'Kinetic Solutions to pictorial Problems: The Films of Man Ray and Moholy-Nagy', in *Artforum* X/1, September 1971.

Scharf, Aaron, *Art and Photography*, London 1968; 2nd ed., London and Baltimore, Md., 1974.

Shand, P. Morton, 'New Eyes for Old', in *The Architectural Review* LXXV, London, January 1934.

Straus, Tomas, *Kassák – Ein ungarischer Beitrag zum Konstruktivismus*, Galerie Gmurzinska, Cologne 1975.

Wingler, Hans Maria, *Das Bauhaus 1919–1933, Weimar, Dessau, Berlin und die Nachfolge in Chicago seit 1937*, Bramsche 1975.

NOTES ON THE PLATES

Besides the already 'well-known' photographic work of Moholy-Nagy, the following plates also include examples which hitherto were practically or completely unknown. Almost two-thirds of these plates were deliberately assigned to photographs taken with a camera, and only one-third was allocated to Moholy's 'speciality', the photogram. The photographs with a camera enable one to get a very clear idea of Moholy's anti-professional attitude which excluded a restricted and one-sided style of photographic vision. His way of taking photographs, which has its antecedents in the development of forms in abstract art, frequently suggests rather a delight in a 'new vision' than intentional 'manipulation'. His span stretches from the occasional private snapshot to the freezing of the sudden appearance of spectacular 'views'. To conclude from the great number of photos which exist in part in negative only and have never been evaluated, Moholy, like an enthusiastic amateur, would keep his camera constantly by him and, when he was in the mood for photography, would 'shoot' a whole series of pictures of a single subject. The numerous photos which he brought back from his holidays testify, among other things, to the amateur-like nature of his photographic inspiration.

Confronted with an œuvre of such diversity and hundreds of the most varied photographs, with a fluid boundary between those resulting from chance circumstances, on the one hand, and artistic intention, on the other, making a choice becomes difficult. To produce a catalogue raisonné, as it seemed to suggest itself at first, proved to be an enterprise that could hardly be justified under these conditions. Among the little-known or until now unknown photographs by Moholy there is a surprisingly high number of picturesque, partly humorous, partly almost surrealist pictures, whose common tenor (apart from the purely Constructivist) points to that 'living' element which frequently plays an important part in Moholy's writings. Many of these photographs have been included here because it seemed important at the present time to give greater emphasis to this quality in his work than has been done in the past.

However, the pictures Moholy himself chose for publication and exhibition as representative of his photographic work are obviously the most important. Above all we must mention here the collection of *60 Fotos* by Frans Roh (1930) which includes the greater part of Moholy's pictures shown at the Deutsche Werkbund exhibition, 'Film und Foto', in Stuttgart in 1929; and in addition the photographs Moholy had published in his own books, in periodicals and in illustrated papers. Many photos by Moholy, of a surprisingly high quality, of which the originals sometimes could no longer be found, were in this way 'discovered a second time'. If extraordinarily good prints from Moholy's days were still available, they could be used here for the respective plates in this book. As his friend Beaumont Newhall has told us, Moholy himself attached more weight to the unity of a photographic picture than to the perfectionist detail of a fully hand-made print and would no doubt have agreed to this procedure. Besides, some of the early publications are, as regards tone-gradations, sharpness and cropping, so superior to the re-prints one can obtain today that here, too, apart from exceptional cases, a good print was preferred to a bad 'original'. Other photos by Moholy, except for rare first prints (vintage prints), are spread around many collections, at times, even in the form of reproductions at second and third hand. To catalogue the stock of examples in all its technical variety was not the intention of this book. Only in cases where it seemed to be important for artistic or historical reasons have other examples been listed. In recognition of the fact that photography as a means of reproduction is, in the last analysis, a medium 'without originals', the pictorial documentary result should be given precedence over the object-character in individual cases. Technical information given by particular collectors about their pictures has, of course, been used and is gratefully acknowledged. All dates which I could not verify personally have been incorporated in the notes with an appropriate remark.

The following points should be noted in the context of the notes on the plates, below:

A specific date and/or title is listed only in the case of photographs to which these details were added by Moholy personally (whether an original print or an item reproduced in a publication over which he had control) or by Lucia Moholy at a later date. All data of this kind either inferred or presumed are listed as such; 'n.d.' = no date.
In dimensions cited (given in centimetres or inches) height generally precedes width; some exceptions will be found in information supplied by owners. Most of the photographs and photograms reproduced in the plates are upright in format.
'Repr.' indicates an item reproduced in an important publication, such examples being mostly from Moholy's own lifetime.
'Source' indicates the origin of the photograph reproduced; in some cases other known examples are also listed.
Stamps occurring on the reverse of prints are designated 'a' and 'b', and indicate respectively the words: (a) (moholy-nagy/berlin chbg. 9/ fredericiastr. 27 atelier'; (b) 'foto moholy-nagy'.

In addition, the following abbreviations are used in the notes (for details of English-language publications, both original and in translation, see Bibliography, above):

GEH	International Museum of Photography at George Eastman House, Rochester, N.Y.
Gernsheim Coll.	Gernsheim Collection, Humanities Research Center, University of Texas, Austin.
Hug Coll.	Hattula and Hansruedi Hug-Moholy-Nagy Collection, Zurich.
Klihm Coll.	Dr H. H. Klihm Collection, Munich.
Larson Coll.	William Larson Collection, Philadelphia.
Levy Coll.	The Art Institute of Chicago, Levy Collection.
LM-N	László Moholy-Nagy.
Lucia M	Lucia Moholy.
MFF	LM-N, *Malerei Fotografie Film*, 2nd revised ed., 1927; cf. *MPF*, below.
MOMA	Museum of Modern Art, New York.
MPF	LM-N, *Malerei Photographie Film* (Bauhaus Book no. 8), 1925; cf. *MFF*, above.
Roh	Franz Roh, *60 Fotos Moholy-Nagy*, Berlin 1930.
Sibyl M-N	Sibyl Moholy-Nagy.
Telehor	Special number of *Telehor* devoted to LM-N, Brno 1936.
Von M zu A	LM-N, *Von Material zu Architektur* (Bauhaus Book no. 14), 1929.

1 At coffee ('bei mokka'), n.d.
Source: Larson Coll., described as '28·6 × 21 cm'; on the verso, stamps 'a | b' and inscribed 'bei mokka'

2 Doll, 1926
Taken at Ascona in 1926 when Moholy and his wife spent a holiday there with the family of Oskar Schlemmer.
This shows clearly Moholy's technique of 'superimposing' different light projections, causing the perception of space to become confused. The shadow of the fence is formally equal to the fence itself, but does not belong to the central camera perspective. This makes the doll lying on the floor look as if it were 'floating'.
Source: Roh, no. 1.

Two Dolls (inset, below) was taken on the same occasion as pl. 2.
Repr.: LM-N, 'Photographie ist Lichtgestaltung', in *Photographische Korrespondenz*, 1 May 1928, fig. 5, with title 'In der Mittagssonne' (In the midday sun). Also in: 'Die "enfesselte kamera" und die "produktive fotografie". Zu den Ideen Professor Moholy-Nagys' by W. Warstadt, in *Deutscher Kamera-Almanach 1929*, p. 45; *Uhu*, June 1929, as 'Puppen im Sonnenbad' (Dolls taking a sun bath); *MFF* (1927) and English ed., where it appears on p. 92 with the caption 'The organization of light and shade, the criss-crossing of the shadows, removes the toy into the realm of the fantastic.'; LM-N, 'Photographie ist Lichtgestaltung' in *Bauhaus* 2, 1928, p. 5.
Source: GEH, described as '48·6 × 38·4 cm "dolls 1925"'.

LM-N, *Two Dolls* (cf. pl. 2).

Portrait of Oskar Schlemmer.

3 The Schlemmer children, 1926
(title according to information supplied orally by Lucia Moholy)
For dating cf. pl. 2.
Repr.: Roh, no. 6.
Source: GEH.

4 Untitled, n.d.
(Lucia Moholy at the breakfast table, about 1926)
Here, the typical circle and cross of the Suprematist symbolism appear against the white ground (as introduced in painting by Malevich; cf. fig. 22 in the introductory text).
Source: Private Coll.; modern print from an old negative.

5 Untitled, n.d.
(Ascona 1926 or La Sarraz 1928; cf. pl. 8)
Moholy photographed his own shadow from the church wall. The 'Suprematist' cross strengthens the impression of a spatial projection in depth, resulting in an almost artistic sensation of floating in space. Through the involvement of the human silhouette the shadow perspective appears more 'real' than the central photographic perspective.
Source: Private Coll.; modern print from an old negative.

Pl. 5

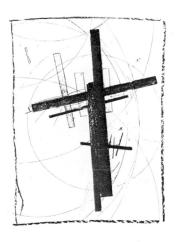

El Lissitzky, *Black ball*, n.d.

K. Malevich, Suprematist drawing, 1917.

Newspaper photo showing a crowd being addressed by loudspeaker, and (right) a graphic rendering by LM-N of the loudspeaker address, pencil and pen and ink, 1924. Both pictures are taken from *Bauhaus 1919–1928*, Stuttgart 1955, pp. 196f. (see Bibliography).

6 Untitled, n.d.
(Lucia Moholy on a balcony)
This picture, too, was probably taken in the Tessin (Ticino), about 1926. In contrast to the predilection for Constructivist structures, here the shifting forms are the chief point of interest: the arabesques of wrought iron and the arrangement of the written characters around the figure almost in the shape of the sails of a windmill.
Source: Levy Coll., described as '34·8 × 25 cm'; signed on verso; stamps 'a + b'.

7 Decorating work, 1925
This plate shows the original area (i.e. as exhibited by Moholy). In the Roh version (cf. fig. 19) the picture was so severely cropped to the right and at the base that the white surface of the house presents the actual background which, because of the projection of telephone wires, becomes unintelligible as a plane. Seen in this way, the decorator painting the façade, in a bizarre and dangerous position, becomes a floating artiste.
Repr.: Roh, no. 59 (cropped at right and below), as 'Entkörpertes Haus' (disembodied house).
Source: Verband ungarischer Fotokünstler (Association of Hungarian photo-artists), Budapest (inv. no. 63.124), described as '39·0 × 30·0 cm. Mounting 1920–1930'.
Other examples: Bauhaus-Archiv, Berlin; Museum of Fine Arts, Boston, Mass., as 'Decorating work, Switzerland 1925'; Klihm Coll. (print reversed), described as 'Switzerland 1925'.

8 Untitled, n.d.
(At the Château La Sarraz, 1928)
In the linear background scheme of the 'counter-composition' a great number of 'surface treatments', 'textures' and structures come into play, making the oblique light seem almost tangible. The picture derives its actual depth from the surface of the water with its crystal-like transparency. Here as so often, Moholy places a small figure in the picture at the precise point that is to become the reference point for the composition.

'La Sarraz' is a château near Lausanne where the annual meetings of avant-garde artists and architects took place (cf. Sibyl M-N, *Experiment in Totality*, pp. 75ff.). From 1927 Moholy spent every summer at La Sarraz.
Source: Private Coll.; modern print from an old negative. An almost identical photograph with the note 'La Sarraz Castle 1928' is in GEH.

9 Untitled, n.d.
(At the Château La Sarraz, 1928–30)
The figure in the background is reminiscent of Xanti Schawinsky, whom Herbert Bayer photographed at La Sarraz as the 'smoking knight' in 1930 (H. Bayer, *Photographic Works*, Los Angeles 1977, figs. 28–29). Moholy took his photograph from roof level (from the tower seen in G. Augsburg's photograph 'Moholy at "La Sarraz", 1932' – see Sibyl M-N, *Experiment in Totality*, p. 76).
Source: Private Coll.; modern print from an old negative.

10 Stockholm, n.d. (1930)
In 1930 Moholy travelled with Ellen Frank in Scandinavia; this photograph must have been taken on this trip.
A very similar photo from the same viewpoint, described as 'Stockholm Photo Moholy-Nagy', was printed in *Querschnitt* no. 5, 1932, p. 328.
Source: Larson Coll.

11 Helsinki, n.d. (1930)
For dating cf. pl. 10.
The date '1927' given by Klihm is not derived from Moholy's own hand, but was provided later by Sibyl M-N. On only one occasion did Moholy experiment with the twofold superimposition of the same picture. The effect becomes film-like and, by the impression of double vision, produces a feeling of giddiness.
Source: Klihm Coll.; 29·7 × 39·2 cm.

12 Marseilles, 1929
Source: Larson Coll., as '9$\frac{11}{16}$ × 6$\frac{15}{16}$', and inscribed on verso 'L. Moholy-Nagy, Rue Cannebierre (Marseille) France'.

13 Belle-Ile-en-Mer, 1925
The 'textures' are very strongly reminiscent of similar formations of stripes in paintings by Alfred Forbat in 1920 and 1923 (cf. K. Passuth,[1] figs. 105, 106). Moholy himself had also, in his early days, painted bird's-eye views of fields (cf. *László Moholy-Nagy*, Stuttgart 1974, figs. 5, 9).
Repr.: Moholy-Nagy, 'La photographie ce qu'elle était, ce qu'elle devra être', *Cahiers d'Art* 4, 1929, p. 31, with caption 'Champs à Belle-Ile-en-Mer. Nous devons au cubisme de trouver des procédés de la facture non seulement des éléments constructeurs mais déjà des expériences'.

1 Krisztina Passuth, *Magyar müvészek as európai avantgarde – ban 1919–1925*, Budapest, 1974.

Source: Hug Coll., after an old 6×9 contact print with Moholy's own inscription 'Belle-Ile-en-uer Juli, 1925 vom leuchtturm' (from the lighthouse).

Pl. 13

Alfred Forbat, *Composition*, 1924

Pl. 14

General view of one of the double houses by Gropius. Photo Lucia Moholy. This general view appeared on p. 134 of Gropius' book *Bauhausbauten Dessau* (Bauhaus Book no. 12, 1930). There, it was described thus: 'The feeling of space changes. While cultural developments of former times embodied in buildings a heavy, solidly monolithic effect . . . and individual interiors, the works of influential present-day architects display an altered sense of space that reflects movement – the traffic of our times – in a fluidity of the total design and the spaces, and seeks to retain the connection between the interior space and the overall space – something that is ruled out by a containing wall.'

14 Untitled, n.d.
(Dessau, 1926–28)
This view is from the second storey of one of the double houses built by Walter Gropius for members of the staff at the Bauhaus; it shows the balcony and the ground-level terrace on the east side. From 1926 to 1928 Moholy shared one of these double houses with Lyonel Feininger.
This picture could be described as a prime example of 'open-air' living and the free penetration of internal and external space proposed for the 'new building'. The regularity of Gropius' architectural design also provides architectonic horizontal and vertical relationships in terms of the movements of people.
Repr.: Roh, no. 56, as 'Vertikalsicht' (vertical view).
Source: Larson Coll., with note of size $(9\frac{3}{4} \times 7\frac{1}{4})$ and inscribed on reverse 'L. Moholy-Nagy'.

15 Untitled, n.d.
(Pipes on a building site, about 1925)
The forms – Suprematist as well as Constructivist – which can be seen here could not but attract Moholy's eye: circle, cross-beams and the projection of their shadows in space.
Even if Moholy cannot match Lissitzky's bold spatial ideas, his vision still differs significantly from the indifference of any photographs of such a subject as seen in

Pl. 15

Otto Erhard Coswig, an example of the New Objectivity in *Der Photofreund*, 1931.

terms of the New Objectivity (see figure). In the example shown here, light and shadow constitute a soft and ornamental arch around the concrete bodies and form delicate outlines of light. In contrast, Moholy does not look at the 'lighting' but at the entire complex of forms transposed into varying degrees of brightness, from which he composes a 'picture'.
Source: *Cahiers d'Art* 4, 1929, p. 33, in the essay by Moholy-Nagy, 'La photographie ce qu'elle était, ce qu'elle devra être'.

16 Bauhaus Balconies at Dessau, n.d. (1926–28)
What was said in the note on pl. 14 applies even more here: the new architecture wants to activate man for the 'conquest of space' (cf. p. 30). Moholy's theatre and ballet work at that same time was based on similar ideas about the spatial quality of human motion.
Source: Bauhaus-Archiv, Berlin.

17 In the stadium, Lyons, n.d. (1929?)
Probably taken in the course of Moholy's journey to Marseilles in 1929.
Source: Larson Coll., described as '$9\frac{1}{4} \times 6\frac{7}{8}$', and inscribed on verso 'Im Stadion von Lyon/Foto Moholy-Nagy'; stamps 'a + b'.

18 The Diving Board, n.d.
As in pl. 14, Moholy emphasizes in this counter-composition both the vertical and horizontal directions in the relationship of the two pairs of legs. This coming together in space of similar figures produces a rather kinetic effect which has its witty explanation in reality in the confrontation of the footprint with the sole of a foot. He who had been standing up is now lying down.
Source: MOMA, described as '$11\frac{1}{8} \times 8\frac{1}{8}$. The Diving Board, n.d.'

19 Reinforced Concrete plane, Ascona, 1928
Source: GEH, described as '$49\cdot7 \times 40$ cm Reinforced concrete plane, Ascona 1928'.

20 Untitled, n.d.
(Hotel terrace, Belle-Ile-en-Mer, 1925)
Sigfried Giedion wrote about this (or a similar) picture: '. . . Belle-Ile-en-Mer, an island off the coast of Brittany. I had spent my first vacation with Moholy there in 1925. I remembered the long conversations in the isolated hotel where we had first clarified what had to be achieved in our time. I remember Moholy taking a photograph of the terrace from a window high above it which annulled the perspective as it forced objects and proportions into the two-dimensional plane. No interesting motif – this concrete slab, a railing, a few chairs, a round table. But it was a completely new beginning. The camera had never been used like that before.' (from Sibyl M-N, *Experiment in Totality*, pp. 93ff.); a similar text by Giedion in *Telehor* (cf. text p. 34).
Source: MFF (1927), p. 91; English edition, p. 93, with caption 'The charm of the photograph lies not in the

object but in the view from above and in the balanced relationships'.

21 'New Year's Morning', n.d. (about 1930)
From the window of his home in Berlin Moholy frequently photographed the street below. This shot, which appeared in an Ullstein illustrated paper, has a slightly artificial character and might even have been posed intentionally.
Source: *Uhu*, vol. 4, 1931, p. 63, as 'Neujahrsmorgen. Aufnahme Moholy-Nagy'.

22 Street paving, 1929
Even more starkly that in pl. 19, the workers are overwhelmed by the site and building materials, and can only just be seen, like tiny ants: the heaps of stone look as if they had come into being by themselves. The forms of work appear, photographically speaking, merely as the attractive composition of various surface treatments and structures in the overall geometry of the road.
Source: GEH, described as '$35 \times 26\cdot7$ cm Street paving 1929'.

23 Untitled, 1928
(Berlin, 1928)
Source: GEH, described as 'Spring Berlin, 1928 (Christmas-Card) 48×38 cm'.

24 Bauhaus Balconies, 1926
Moholy reproduced this photograph in *MFF* (1927); cf. English ed., p. 60, with caption 'The optical truth of the perspectival construction'. Like the Russian artists, Moholy, too, aimed at optical 'objectivity' without 'our eye complementing optical phenomena through our intellectual experience of formal and spatial associations'. B. Arvatov wrote in 1926: 'Present-day art-school leavers are half-educated specialists who, for instance, do not look at perspective from the point of view of analytical and descriptive geometry, i.e. from an elementary scientific point of view, but from that of optical perception.' (B. Arvatov, *Kunst und Produktion*, Munich 1972, p. 20).
All the same, Moholy creates new associations: the photo 'lays flat' the wall of the house in such a way that one can apparently walk up a staircase without having – as would be necessary in a real situation – to raise one's head.
Repr.: *MFF*, p. 58 (English ed., p. 60).
Source: GEH, described as '$49\cdot5 \times 39\cdot3$ cm Bauhaus balconies Worm's-eye view 1926'.

25 Untitled, n.d.
(Sibyl Moholy-Nagy in London, about 1936)
In order to earn a living in London, Moholy worked on shop-window displays. (cf. Sibyl M-N, *Experiment in Totality*, pp. 119ff.). The photo shows the new dimension of a mixture of artistic and commercial aesthetics (cf. note 117, p. 43).
Source: Hug Coll.; modern print from an old negative.

26 Untitled, n.d.
Source: Private Coll.; modern print from an old negative.

27 The Pavilion Bexhill on Sea, 1936
The Pavilion at Bexhill on Sea was built by Erich Mendelsohn. The photo shows the concept of 'space' in 'new building', which Moholy described in his book *Von M zu A* (cf. English ed., pp. 56ff.).
Source: Klihm Coll., 21·6 × 16·7 cm.

28 The Pavilion, Bexhill on Sea, 1936
For style, compare pl. 107.
Source: Private Coll.; modern print from an old negative.

29 Untitled, n.d.
(View of the Hohenzollern Bridge from the Cologne Fair)
For dating cf. pl. 36.
Source: Private Coll.; modern print from an old negative.

30 Notre Dame, Paris, 1925
In 1925 Moholy was in Paris together with the architectural historian, Sigfried Giedion. In 1928 Giedion published his book *Bauen in Frankreich, Bauen in Eisen und Eisenbeton* ('Building in France, Building in cast iron and in reinforced concrete') which traced — as did Viollet-le-Duc — the historical development of architectural functionalism right back to gothic rib vaulting. This nineteenth-century 'functionalist' concept of the Gothic Age may also have motivated Moholy when he took his photograph of the cathedral which, in a curious technical way, shows what looks like a skyscraper. The columns shoot like tubes through a shaft and the modern water tank is one of the most significant elements of the picture. Hardly any essential difference exists between this and one of Moholy's pictures of actual pipes. It is best

compared to a photograph by Walter Scherz: the Woolworth Building in New York seen from a zeppelin (*Uhu*, July 1925, p. 21).
Repr.: *Querschnitt*, 12, 1930.
Source: Hug Coll.; reproduction after an old 6 × 9 print with stamp 'a'; another example in MOMA, described as 'Notre Dame de Paris 1925'.

31 Untitled, n.d.
(Building of the locomotive shed at Bagneux near Paris, 1925?)
The loco-shed (by Eugène Freyssinet) is illustrated in Sigfried Giedion's *Time, Space, Architecture*, 8th ed., nos. 219 b, c, and dated 1929. Cf. also Giedion's *Bauen in Frankreich, Bauen in Eisen und Eisenbeton*. The photograph was probably taken in 1925 when Moholy was in Paris with Giedion. By the time of Moholy's second stay in Paris, in 1929/30, the shed had already been completed.
Source: Verband ungarischer Fotokünstler (Association of Hungarian photo-artists), Budapest, inv. no. 58, described as '38 × 32 cm Konstruktion 1922'.

32 Eiffel Tower, 1925
The unusual curves in the upper half of the picture result from the Citroën sign which at that time covered the entire height of the tower. Quite unfunctionalistically and purely from the point of view of the picture, Moholy united in one composition these applied forms with the curves of the railings and achieved in this way the striking spatial effect of depth.
Source: Klihm Coll., 29·2 × 22 cm; inscribed on verso 'Eiffelturm 1925', and stamp 'a'.

33 Untitled, n.d.
(Pont Transbordeur, Marseilles 1929)
Negative print. Cf. note to pl. 41.
Source: Klihm Coll.; 18 × 23·8 cm.

34 Untitled, n.d.
(Eiffel Tower, 1925)
Source: Hug Coll.; reproduction after a 6 × 9 print bearing stamp 'moholy-nagy', expanded in Moholy's hand to read 'foto moholy-nagy'.

35 Untitled, n.d.
(Water slide at the bathing pool, Zurich, 1920?)
Title and date are taken from a print in Budapest (see below). There is, however, no proof that Moholy had taken photographs before 1922; nor is there any evidence for such an early journey by Moholy to Zurich. On the other hand, this early — still Dadaist — dating can be regarded as possible by analogy with Moholy's early paintings and related works by Schwitters.
Source: Verband ungarischer Fotokünstler, Budapest, inv. no. 68.707, described as 'Wasserrutschbahn in dem Zürcher Strandbad, 1920, 25·5 × 17·7 cm'.
Another example: Kunstbibliothek, Staatliche Museen Stiftung Preußischer Kulturbesitz, Berlin (West), inv. no. 29.152.

Pl. 30.

L. Moholy-Nagy, *Pipes*
(reproduced in Roh, no. 49).

PI. 35

L. Moholy-Nagy, *Bridges*, oil, 1920.

Kurt Schwitters, *Industrial zone*, drawing, 1920.

36 Untitled, n.d.
(The Hohenzollern Bridge, Cologne, seen from the Fairground, 1927–29)
This photograph and pl. 29 must date from the same journey, i.e. between 1927 (completion of the tower at the Cologne Fair) and 1929, the year of photographic exhibition (Internationale Film- und Fotoausstellung) in Stuttgart, from which Franz Roh selected material for his book *Moholy-Nagy 60 Fotos*.
Source: Roh, no. 5.

37 Untitled, n.d.
(View from the Berlin Radio Tower, before 1928)
There are at least four similar photographs from the same viewpoint which amount to a sort of all-round view from the tower; it may be assumed that these photographs were all taken on the same day.
Repr.: *Querschnitt*, May 1931.
Source: Hug Coll., after an old contact print 6 × 8·3 cm; on verso, in Moholy's own hand, 'L. Moholy-Nagy'.
Similar examples: Bauhaus-Archiv; also MOMA, with date '1928'.

38 Radio Tower, Berlin, n.d.
This photograph can be dated between September 1926

(the opening of the Radio Tower) and its first publication, on 1 May 1928.
Repr.: LM-N, 'Photographie ist Lichtgestaltung' (Photography is Manipulation of Light) in *Photographische Korrespondenz*, 1 May 1928, p. 136, fig. 6. Also in *Qualität* IX, 1/2, 1931.
Source: *Das neue Berlin* 1, January 1929, p. 3.

39 Untitled, n.d.
(View from the Berlin Radio Tower in winter, 1928)
A number of similar photographs, including this one and pl. 40, form what amounts to a series; others are in the Levy Collection, Chicago, and MOMA, New York, the latter being dated 1928.
Source: Hug Coll.

40 Untitled, n.d.
(View from the Berlin Radio Tower in winter, 1928)
Repr.: *Telehor*, no. 52, dated 1928; also *Vision in Motion*, fig. 226, dated 1928.
Source: Klihm Coll., 19 × 24·8 cm; on the verso 'From the radiotower Berlin 1928', and (in Moholy's own hand) 'L. Moholy-Nagy'.
Other examples: MOMA, dated 1928; Gernsheim Coll.

41 Untitled, n.d.
(View from the Pont Transbordeur, Marseilles, 1929)
In 1929 Moholy went to Marseilles. The steel Pont Transbordeur is a transporter bridge, built by Arnodin in 1905. It had first come to the attention of Sigfried Giedion as a precursor of modern spatial construction, and he was also the first to take pictures of it. He published some of these in 1927 in the periodical *Der Cicerone*, where he wrote about the example reproduced here: 'A view from the narrow walkway situated up high, down to the suspended ferry. A multitude of new possibilities of looking, everything is founded on mobility.' In 1928 Giedion's book *Bauen in Frankreich, Bauen in Eisen, Bauen in Eisenbeton* appeared, where it is stated apropos the 'New Building': 'There exists only one large indivisible space, dominated by relationships and penetrations in

PI. 41

Pont Transbordeur, photograph by Sigfried Giedion, reproduced in his article 'Zur Situation der französischen Architektur II', in *Der Cicerone*, 1927.

place of delimitations . . . our attitude of today demands of a house the best possible overcoming of heaviness. Light dimensions. Openings. Space flooded by air. Things that were first suggested by the constructive creations of the last century. The point has been reached when building takes its place in the general process of life.'

Thus the Pont Transbordeur had become, after the Eiffel Tower, another precursor of the avant-garde of the 1920s and was visited by numerous artists, among them also photographers like Germaine Krull, Herbert Bayer and Florence Henri, who created through their numerous photographs a modernist 'aura' around this until then unknown structure.

Source: Hug Coll.; reproduced from an old 6 × 9 print.

42 View from the Pont Transbordeur, Marseilles, 1929

Here it becomes specially clear that Moholy − in contrast, for instance, to Giedion's conventional photographs (cf. illustration) − wants to show, by the superimposition of grades of brightness, new spatial relationships that cannot be achieved by perspective effects. At times he almost achieves the abstract quality of his photograms.

Pl. 42

L. Moholy-Nagy, Photogram.

Source: GEH, described as '40 × 36 cm, From the Transporter Bridge, Marseille 1929'.

43 View from the Pont Transbordeur, Marseilles, 1929

Source: GEH, described as '49·9 × 40 cm. View from the Pont Transbordeur, Marseille, Iron Column. 1929'.

44 Untitled, n.d.

(In the old port of Marseilles, 1929)
At the top of the picture one can just see one of the round foundations supporting the main structure of the Pont Transbordeur, and around which some boats are moored.
Source: *Qualität* IX, 1/2, 1931.

45 Boats in the old port of Marseilles, 1929

A similar photograph had been taken earlier by Herbert Bayer but his view remained more sober and 'graphic'. In contrast to this, Moholy, delighting in the colourful variety of the types of boat, is both 'richer' and, through the diagonal 'counter-composition', more severe in his arrangement than Bayer.
Source: GEH, described as '50·4 × 40 cm Boats in the old harbour of Marseille 1929'.

46 Boats in the old port of Marseilles, 1929

This photograph was first published by Moholy in the periodical *Qualität* in 1931, but there the image was reversed (cf. pl. 45).
Source: *Qualität* IX, 1/2, 1931.

Pl. 46

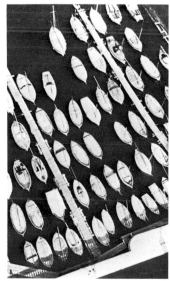

Herbert Bayer, *The small harbour, Marseilles*, 1928.

47 Untitled, n.d.

(View from the Pont Transbordeur, Marseilles, 1929)
This picture closes Moholy's series on this subject. Constructivist photography sought to grasp the object, by taking a series of shots from all sides (cf. note 103, p. 43). However, Moholy allows his eye to rove freely and thus

Pl. 47

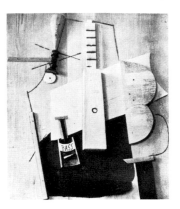

Picasso, *Wooden relief*, 1913 (mentioned by LM-N in *Von M zu A*, p. 82; English ed., p. 36).

obtains from his chosen viewpoint the most varied results (cf. text, pp. 29ff.).
Here he captures a composition which is reminiscent of Picasso's pictures and like them has aspects that are both mysterious and visionary.
Repr.: *Qualitat* IX, 1/2, 1931.
Source: Levy Coll. (C44052), 29·5 × 25 cm

48 Untitled, n.d.
(Journey to Scandinavia, 1930)
In 1930 Moholy travelled with Ellen Frank in Scandinavia (cf. the catalogue of the Levy Collection, Chicago, 1976, p. 83); the date is also corroborated by the Helsinki picture (pl. 11).
Source: Private Coll.; modern print from an old negative.

49 Untitled, n.d.
(Journey to Scandinavia, 1930)
Source: Private Coll.; modern print from an old negative.

50 Untitled, n.d.
(Journey to Scandinavia, 1930)
Source: Larson Coll., as '24·2 × 18 cm', with, on verso, Moholy's description 'fotoreporterin im nördlichen eis-meer' (woman photo-reporter in the Arctic Ocean).

51 Untitled, n.d.
(Journey to Scandinavia, 1930)
Source: Private Coll.; modern print from an old negative.

52 Untitled, n.d.
(Journey to Scandinavia, 1930)
Sources: Klihm Coll.; Bauhaus-Archiv, Berlin, under the title 'Laufsteg von oben' (gangplank from above), 24·5 × 17·6 cm., dated by Sibyl M-N in her own hand '1926'.

53 Untitled, n.d.
(Journey to Scandinavia, 1930)
Source: Larson Coll., 24·2 × 17·2 cm, inscribed by Moholy

'am molo erwartet man nun die fischer ungeduldig Finnland Photo Moholy-Nagy (der fisch trocknet).' [on the jetty the fishermen are impatiently awaited, Finland, ... (the fish are drying)].

54 Untitled, n.d.
(Journey to Scandinavia, 1930)
Source: Private Coll.; modern print from an old negative.

55 Negative, n.d. (before 1927)
Repr.: Roh, no. 15; LM-N, 'fotografie ist lichtestaltung', in *Bauhaus*, 1928, p. 6; *MFF* (1927), p. 96 (English ed., p. 98, with caption 'The transposition of the tone-values transposes the relationships too. The small amount of white becomes most strikingly visible and so determines the character of the whole picture.').
Source: Levy Coll.

56 Portrait, n.d.
(Ellen Frank, about 1929)
Photographing a face in close-up constitutes one of the typical photographic methods which at that time were also discovered in cinema. Moholy's trick is to direct the eye away from this close proximity into an indeterminate distance by means of the brilliantly shining mirror of the eyeball. The distortion of the proportions is also remi-niscent of the Dada collages of faces by Hannah Höch. Only an 'elemental' concept of art could fragment the conventional unity of a face to such a degree.
Repr.: Roh, no. 16, with caption 'Durch äußerste Nähe höchste Großform' (Maximum size through extreme closeness).
Source: Kunstbibliothek, Staatliche Museen Stiftung Preußischer Kulturbesitz, Berlin (West), acquired by the library in 1929.

57 Portrait, n.d.
(Vladimir Mayakovsky, 1924)
According to Hubertus Gassner this is a portrait of the Russian poet Vladimir Mayakovsky who visited Berlin several times; Moholy can only have met him at the earliest in 1924, after having got in touch with him through Mayakovsky's friend A. Rodchenko whom he met in 1923.
Mayakovsky, the founder of LEF (the 'left front' of the arts) was also the most important representative of LEF artists in the West. Thus the photo is an important document for Moholy's contact with Russian artists. Mayakovsky, who was only two years older than Moholy, committed suicide in 1930. Perhaps the fact that the portrait of Mayakovsky is the last picture in Roh's book is a hidden tribute to the artist.
Source: Roh, no. 60, with caption 'Großform gegen das Licht' (Large form against the light).

58 Portrait, n.d.
(Lucia Moholy, 1924?)
Lucia Moholy's verbal suggestion for the probable date of this portrait is 1927.

Source: Kunstbibliothek, Staatliche Museen Stiftung Preußischer Kulturbesitz, Berlin (West), inv. no. 29.152, size 38 × 28·5 cm.
Another example: Hug Coll., described as 'Bildnis Porträt Lucia 1924'.

59 Portrait, n.d.
Repr.: *Das deutsche Lichtbild*, 1930, p. 23, with caption 'Porträt, Ernemann Kamera 6 × 9, Anastigmat 1 : 4·5, F = 12 cm., Blende 25. Hauff Flavinplatte, belichtet $\frac{1}{100}$ Sek. September mittags, sonnig, vergrössert auf Leonar Bromsilber hart 30 × 40 hochglanz'.
Source: Roh, no. 2, with caption 'Spezifisch fotografische Wirklichkeitsnähe' (specifically photographic closeness to reality).
Another example: Verband ungarischer Fotokünstler, Budapest, inventory no. 75.143, described as 'Portrait 1930 30·3 × 23·6 cm'.

60 Portrait, n.d.
(Lucia Moholy)
The heavy shadow at the left lends the face an almost Cubist quality, with a second silhouette, rather like the 'cimultaneous portrait' of Hannah Höch illustrated by Moholy in *MFF* (1927), p. 96 (English ed., p. 99).
Repr.: LM-N, 'La photographie ce qu'elle était, ce qu'elle devra être', *Cahiers d'Art*, 4, 1929, p. 28; Roh, no. 48, where the caption notes that special lighting and flattening make the head appear as if masked.
Source: MOMA.

61 Portrait, n.d.
Negative print.
Repr.: Roh, no. 21, with caption 'Negativ'.
Source: MOMA.

62 Portrait of Solomon Guggenheim, n.d. (about 1926)
This photograph was probably taken in Ascona, where Guggenheim made several visits and, together with Hilla Rebay, had cultivated contacts with European artists. In this way it came about that Moholy sold his first paintings to the Guggenheim Collection.
Source: Klihm Coll., 26·6 × 18 cm.; signed 'M = N', and inscribed 'S. G. der Kupferkönig [the copper king], New York 1928'.

63 Portrait, n.d.
Source: Roh, no. 41.

64 Portrait, n.d.
Repr.: Sibyl M-N, *Experiment in Totality*, 1969, fig. 8, as 'Market Woman, ca. 1923'.
Source: Klihm Coll., with a (questionable) inscription 'Olga Werefkin, 1920'.

65 Portrait, n.d.
Negative print of pl. 64.
Source: Klihm Coll.

66 Portrait, n.d.
(Lucia Moholy, 1925)
Probably taken on Belle-Ile-en-Mer where Lucia and László Moholy-Nagy spent their holiday with Giedion and his wife in 1925. Perhaps Moholy had been influenced by Surrealist tendencies in Paris shortly before.
Source: Larson Coll., described as 'Portrait of Lucia Moholy, modern print from original negative 1925'.

67 Portrait, n.d.
This photo (which, in its treatment of shadows, is somewhat reminiscent of pl. 61) was given the date 1920 by Beke (cf. László Beke, 'László Moholy-Nagy, "The Light Artist"', in *Interpressgrafik*, Budapest, no. 1, 1977, p. 65). There is no valid evidence for this dating, since the wording on the Budapest original (see below) cannot be regarded as reliable.
Repr.: *Uhu*, May 1928, with caption 'Die erste heiße Sonnenstunde' (the first hour of hot sun); Roh, no. 8.
Source: MOMA, no. 478.39, described as 'Repose, n.d.'; another example, Verband ungarischer Fotokünstler, Budapest, inv. no. 58.165, as 'Die Ruhe 1920. 28 × 21 cm'.

68 Two nudes, 1927–29
This photograph was taken on the same occasion as pl. 69, the figure in the background being the same.
Source: GEH, described as 'Two nudes 1925, 27·4 × 36·7 cm'; another example, formerly Klihm Coll., Munich, with date '1927' possibly in LM-N's own hand.

69 Negative of Nude, 1927–29
The frequent negative rendering of pictures of nudes corresponds, as in the portraits, to Moholy's tendency to keep 'visual experience' free from any intellectual harmony and association. Like Renoir's use of light-play around bodies, so Moholy's photograph reveals patches of light adapting the curves of the body, sublimating tactile into optical sensation.

L. Moholy-Nagy, *Nude* (positive and negative as reproduced in *Telehor*), 1929.

Repr.: *Telehor*, no. 47 (reversed), together with a positive print of the same picture and caption '1. moholy-nagy 1929 fotografie (positiv und negativ)'.
Source: MOMA, no. 504.39, described as 'Nude 1929'.

70 Portrait of Ellen Frank, 1929
Cf. text, p. 35.
Source: Hug Coll., 40·3 × 30·5 cm.; verso inscribed by Moholy 'ellen (sellin) 1929', and stamp 'a'.

71 Untitled (about 1927)
Probably taken on the same occasion as pl. 72.
Repr.: *Arts et Métiers Graphiques*, 1930; *Deutche Kunst und Dekoration*, vol. 70, 1932 (in the article by Dr Alfred Kuhn, 'Die Ausstellung "Das Meisterphoto"', pp. 245ff.).
Source: GEH, described as 'Sailing 1926, 47·2 × 27·2 cm'.

72 Boat under tow, 1927.
Negative print.
Repr.: *Arts et Métiers Graphiques*, 1930 (as positive); Roh, no. 12, with the positive version of the same picture and caption referring to the 'revaluation and enhancement of the previous one [i.e. the positive print]'; *Bauhaus 1919–28*, Stuttgart 1955, with date '1927'.
Source: Klihm Coll., 38·7 × 29 cm.; another example in Levy Coll., with date '1927'.

73–74 Nude:
positive – negative, 1931
Source: Klihm Coll., the inscription 'Moholy-Nagy 31' is in the hand of Sibyl M-N; another example in GEH.

75 Untitled, n.d. (end of the 1920s)
This photo, hardly more than a snapshot, resembles contemporary illustrations in comic papers: the idea of the 'lovable crowd' frequently encountered from the end of the 1920s in many illustrated papers, acts as a petty-bourgeois contrast to politicized masses.
Source: Private Coll., modern print from an old negative.

76 Untitled, n.d.
(Beach near Sellin, 1929)
This photograph and pl. 77 were both taken in the evening at the same spot – from a wooden tower on the beach.
Source: MOMA, described as 'Sand architects No. 2 n.d. $11\frac{3}{8} \times 8\frac{1}{4}$'.

77 Untitled, n.d.
(On the beach at Sellin, 1929)
The date may be established from pl. 70, as the photo is likely to have been taken during the same stay at Sellin. As in pl. 5, the photographer brings his own shadow into the picture (top left). The issue of *Uhu* for October 1929 includes a very similar picture with the caption: 'In my photos I have nearly always worked without a pre-meditated plan. But all the same my photographs are not the result of chance. I have learnt to grasp a given situation quickly. Therefore when the relationships of light and shadow strongly impressed me, I have fixed the segment

which appeared to be most favourable. This beach picture is the result of this method.'
Source: *die neue linie*, September 1929, p. 40; the caption reads 'The shadows are becoming longer. The actress Ellen Frank on the beach at Sellin. Photograph Moholy-Nagy.'

78 Untitled, n.d. (1929?)
Source: Kunstbibliothek, Staatliche Museen Stiftung Preußischer Kulturbesitz, Berlin (West), inv. no. 29.152, 38 × 28·5 cm (acquired 1929).

79 Untitled, n.d. (1929?)
Probably taken on the same occasion as pl. 76.
Source: MOMA, described as 'Play n.d., $14\frac{1}{8} \times 10\frac{3}{8}$'.

80 Untitled, n.d. (1929?)
The picture shows the same children as in pl. 79. The graininess of the print shows that it is a much enlarged detail. This is one of the very rare cases in which Moholy really manipulated a detail of a picture. Usually he retained the original intact.
Source: Roh, no. 32, with caption 'Fotografische Unmittelbarkeit des Augenblicks' (Photographic immediacy of the moment).

81 Fishbones, 1930
To use Moholy's terminology, the effect here is one of 'massing' (see *Von M zu A*, p. 48; English ed., p. 26). Moholy is not interested in the usual lighting effects which made such pictures of fish popular with the photography of the New Objectivity. He is as always only interested in the transposition of real forms into degrees of brightness and the structural elements that create an effect in pictures. He is fascinated by formations that are self-generated and do not require to be arranged to produce suitable subjects.
Source: GEH, described as 'fish bones, Norway 1930', 37·4 × 26 cm.

82 Wistaria, n.d. (1924?)
An example of Moholy's almost surrealist interest in the automatism of 'organic' forms. The projection of shadows seems to penetrate the wall of the house.
Source: Hug Coll., 21 × 27·2 cm; on the verso (in LM-N's own hand) 'foto moholy-nagy glyzinienbaum' and (added by Sibyl M-N), 'Locarno 1924'.

83 Ascona, 1926
Here the 'Constructivist' treatment of shadows is super-imposed on the photographic perspective and hides the children almost completely. The bold shadows form their own system of co-ordinates whereby the torso of the tree trunk becomes the most important feature in the picture. The effect is similar to that of the doll in pl. 2, which was also taken in Ascona in 1926.
Repr.: Roh, no. 37.
Source: MOMA, described as 'Ascona 1926 $14\frac{3}{8} \times 10\frac{7}{8}$'; another example in GEH (reversed).

84 Fish-heads 1928
Source: Private Coll.; modern print from an old negative. Another example in Smithsonian Institution, Washington, D.C.; verso signed and dated 1928, with title 'Fischköpfe'.

85 Cat Negative, n.d. (about 1926)
In any photograph the white spaces always produce an 'active' effect. Through the reversal into the negative the shape of the cat's body, normally immediately recognizable, is eliminated, and the internal pattern of the fur becomes the lambent principal feature of the composition. Repr.: *Von M zu A*, p. 40, as 'Textur, das Fell einer Katze'; Roh, no. 18, described as 'Magical effect of the negative'. Also, in positive prints, in: *Arts et Métiers Graphiques*, 1930; *Das deutsche Lichtbild*, 1930, p. 76, with caption 'Katze, Ernemann-Kamera 6 × 9 cm., Anastigmat 1 : 4·5 F = 12 cm., Gevaert Super-sensima-Specialplatte, belichtet 1/50 Sek., September, mittags, sonnig. Vergrössert auf Leonar-Bromsilber, hart 30 × 40 cm, Hochglanz'.
Source: Klihm Coll., 24·7 × 18·8 cm.

86 Castle ruin in the Rhineland, n.d. (1923?)
Here, the aim is not to produce a view, but an area of brightness floating in space, as in a photogram (e.g. pl. 149). The perspective in depth is eliminated.
Source: Klihm Coll., 21·6 × 28·2 cm; inscribed on the verso, 'burgruine (turm) im rheinland/castle ruin' and (in Sibyl M-N's hand) '1928'; stamps 'a + b'.

87 Sewer opening in Paris, 1925
For the date cf. note to pl. 30.
This is a prime model for different surface treatments and 'modulations' of the same basic substance, viz. water. All the physical structures of the picture are transposed into various water-equivalents and from those into radiant light phenomena. Moholy compared the 'element' of water with the 'element' of light several times, e.g. *Von M zu A*, pp. 169–74 (cf. English ed., p. 48).
Repr.: Roh, no. 31, with caption 'Unheimliche Kanalöffnung in Paris'; *Von M zu A*, p. 50. fig. 34 (not in English edition).
Source: GEH, described as '29 × 20·8 cm, culvert 1925'.

88 Hiddensee (1929?)
As noted in pl. 76, Moholy was at Sellin on the island of Rügen in 1929; possibly he also visited the small neighbouring island of Hiddensee. The photograph looks conventional but it shows Moholy's feeling for forms of sand and grass 'automatically' created by the wind. The whole picture could also be called a 'light modulator'.
Source: Hug Coll.; on the verso (in Sibyl M-N's hand) 'L. Moholy-Nagy Düne [dunes] Hiddensee 1930'.

89 Belle-Ile-en-Mer, 1925
Moholy's frequently applied principle of omitting the horizon from his views seen from above compresses all optical phenomena into the picture plane. The broad water surface becomes a glittering curtain.

Repr.: no. 23, demonstrating a 'typically photographic enhancement of the material'.
Source: Private Coll.; on the verso 'Gegenlicht 1926' (probably the handwriting of Sibyl M-N), 'Belle-Ile-en Mer (Bretagne)' (typed on piece of paper), and 'Photo L. Moholy-Nagy' (Moholy's handwriting).

90 Untitled, n.d.
(Beggars, Marseilles harbour, 1929)
For dating cf. notes to pl. 41ff. On closer scrutiny this looks anything but picturesque. The man lying among the rubbish and scattered stones gives the impression of being himself a piece of rubbish thrown down in the street. Moholy created a more profound study of a beggar than did others among his contemporaries. In *Querschnitt*, for example, there appeared the picture (shown here), full of bourgeois romantic ideas of a tramp's life with, in the background, a mean little joke.
The journal *Der Arbeiterfotograf* published — and exhibited several times — a totally formalistic and obviously posed picture which could hide its weakness only behind the caption 'Ruined by the capitalist world order'.
Source: Klihm Coll.; another example, Ex Libris Division of Art, New York, described as 'Marseille, vieux port, 1930 20·6 × 32·2 cm'.

Pl. 90

Emil Straßburg, *Sleeping beggar in Marseilles*, from *Querschnitt*, September 1931.

Ruined by the capitalist world order, from *Der Arbeiterfotograf*, 7, 1930, p. 156.

91 Untitled, n.d.
(Paris, 1925?)
Source: Private Coll.; modern print from an old negative.

92 Untitled, n.d.
(Paris, 1925?)
Source: Private Coll.; modern print from an old negative.

93 Untitled, n.d.
(In Switzerland, second half of the 1920s)
Source: Private Coll.; modern print from an old negative.

94 Untitled, n.d. (1926?)
The manner of composition suggests that this is earlier than the pictures from Marseilles, and is reminiscent of pls. 82 and 83.
Source: Private Coll.; modern print from an old negative.

95 Untitled, n.d.
(Paris, 1925?)
Source: Private Coll.; modern print from an old negative.

96 Untitled, n.d.
(Marseilles, 1929)
Source: Private Coll.; modern print from an old negative.

97 Untitled, n.d.
(Paris 1925 or Marseilles 1929)
Source: Private Coll.; modern print from an old negative.

98 Untitled, n.d.
(Gypsy, Berlin, 1932)
In 1932 Moholy made a film about gypsies in Berlin (cf. Sibyl M-N, *Experiment in Totality*, pp. 78ff). Two illustrations taken from the film (nos. 66, 67) appeared in *Telehor*; they correspond exactly in certain points of detail with this photograph.
Source: Private Coll.; modern print from an old negative.

99 Lapp Woman, 1930
On the basis of Moholy's own handwritten identification, this photo can only have been taken on his Scandinavian trip in 1930.
As early as 1925, Moholy had written (*MPF*, p. 29; Eng. ed., p. 36): 'What a surprise it would be if, for example, it

Pl. 99

A. Rodchenko, film advertisement, 1926.

were possible to film a man daily from birth to his death in old age. It would be most unnerving even to be able to watch only his face with the slowly changing expression of a long life ... all in 5 minutes ...' (cf. note 80, p. 42). In this picture the contrast of the bright eye of the child with the wrinkled brow of the Lapp woman seems to combine such change. Formally speaking, Moholy is here still influenced by Constructivist posters, e.g. those by Rodchenko.
Source: Hug Coll.; on the verso, stamp 'b', (in Moholy's own hand) 'lappenfrau (eismeer)', and (in another hand) 'Moholy-Nagy'.

100 Untitled, n.d.
(Paris 1925)
Source: Hug Coll.; modern print from an old negative.

101 Untitled, n.d.
(Paris, 1925?)
Source: Private Coll.; modern print from an old negative.

102 Untitled, n.d.
(London, 1935–37)
During his stay in England, from 1935 to 1937, Moholy was obliged, for the first time, to treat photography as a source of income. In Germany he had sold his photographs to the press merely because he was interested in seeing them published or because he had received a friendly request. In 1936 he put together a volume of photographs, called *The Street Markets of London*, for publication in England; this was followed in 1937 by *Eton Portrait.* In 1939 there appeared yet another volume called *An Oxford University Chest* (with text by John Betjeman). The somewhat popular humour of this picture may have something to do with new demands of commercial work.
Source: Private Coll.; modern print from an old negative.

103 Untitled, n.d.
(Scandinavia, 1930)
Cf. note to pl. 48.
Source: Private Coll.; modern print from an old negative.

104 Untitled, n.d.
(In the old port at Marseilles, 1929)
Cf. notes to pls. 41–45.
Source: Private Coll.; modern print from an old negative.

105 Untitled, n.d.
(Crevasse, 1931?)
The subject, which is in principle similar to the view in pl. 89, is not clear cut. For Moholy it was important to capture light gradations with a spatial effect. The original perspective depth of the crevasse is re-interpreted (almost in Kandinsky's sense) as an indefinable space (cf. text, p. 24).
Exhibited: Künstlerhaus, Brünn, as 'Glacier' (1935).
Repr.: *Telehor*, no. 53, as 'Fotografie 1931'.
Source: Klihm Coll.; on the verso (in Sibyl M-N's hand) 'Moholy-Nagy 1926 Sewer Berlin'.

106 Laboratory, 1938

After 1930 Moholy's photographic work sometimes had a perfectionist and professional character. This photograph was taken in Chicago.

Source: GEH, 27·1 × 34·7 cm.

107 Light-Space-Modulator

Moholy designed and built this kinetic sculpture or light machine between 1922 and 1930 and exhibited it in 1930 at the Deutsche Werkbund exhibition in Paris (cf. H. Weitemeier, *Lichtvisionen – Ein Experiment von Moholy-Nagy*, Bauhaus-Archiv, Berlin, 1972).

In 1930, several photographs of the apparatus were taken in Paris, by (among others) André Kertesz. In the same year Moholy produced the abstract film *Light Display, Black and White and Grey*, which utilized this sculpture. Sibyl M-N reports (*Experiment in Totality*, p. 66) that Moholy regarded the film as almost more important than the sculpture itself. His aim was the production of an abstract 'light chronology'. The photographic interpretation takes up a position between sculpture and film and suggests the effects seen in photograms (e.g. pl. 142).

The detailed forms of the apparatus are rationalizations in technical language of Cubist-style patterns (e.g. by Juan Gris), in the manner in which Henryk Berlewi propagated them as 'Mechano-Faktur'. Moholy substitutes for Berlewi's rigid arrangement a kinetic and spatial one. The style of the photograph (probably taken with the collaboration of a photographer with a studio camera) is for Moholy unusually professional.

Source: MOMA, described as 'Lightplay Black-White-Grey. $14\frac{11}{16} \times 10\frac{13}{16}$ gift of the photographer. Accepted 12.3.37. 1937.'

Pl. 107

Henryk Berlewi, *Mechano-Faktur*, from *Der Sturm*, 1924.

108–150 Photograms

108 Photogram, 1922

This is the earliest stage in Moholy's work with photograms. Formally, it is entirely independent of Man Ray and obviously represents Moholy's attempt at that time to solve his problems as a painter (the penetration of planes, the elimination of individual handwriting) by means of a new technique of more functional and rational production. Moholy produced at the same time (1922) his Enamel picture (telephone picture), with which the photogram

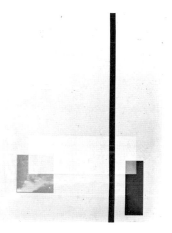

L. Moholy-Nagy, Enamel picture *EM 3*, 1923.

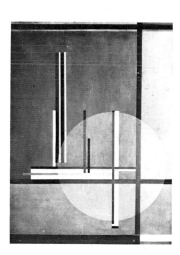

L. Moholy-Nagy, *LIS*, oil painting, 1922.

might be compared. He maintained that he had coined the term 'photogram' by analogy with the word 'telegram' (cf. p. 51). Moholy had used the telephone to convey his instructions (about forms and the arrangement of colours for his telephone picture) to a firm producing enamel signs, and was enthusiastic about the complete separation of material production from intellectual design (cf. Lucia Moholy, *Marginalien*, pp. 32ff.). Indeed, something similar happens in photograms, where light does the work of the

73

material production of the picture from, as it were, a distance.

Source: Smithsonian Institution, Washington, D.C., inv. no. 69.112.5, 13·8 × 8·9 cm; mounted on paper and inscribed below the print 'Moholy-Nagy/1922'; on the verso, signature in pencil and, in ink, 'Lichtgestaltung ohne Camera [light manipulation without a camera] 1922' (some damage to the picture surface near the lower margin).

109 Photogram (1922)
This sheet belongs to the series of four photograms that were the first to be published by Moholy.
Repr.: *Broom*, March 1923.
Source: Smithsonian Institution, Washington, D.C., inv. no. 69.112.2, 14·2 × 10·2 cm, mounted on paper; on the verso, stamp 'L. Moholy-Nagy' and 'Berlin. W. 35/ Lützowstr. 73/IV' (cf. also note to pl. 110).

110 Photogram (1922)
The date 1921 (see below) was probably added later by Sibyl M-N, who presented the Smithsonian Institution with five such sheets (for dates consult Sources, pp. 51f.). The stamp names an address in Berlin which is also that given for Moholy in the periodical *Ma*, whose correspondent he then was. As described by Lucia and László Moholy-Nagy, this photogram was still produced on daylight-sensitive paper and obviously exposed in daylight (cf. p. 51 and Lucia Moholy, *Marginalien – Marginal Notes*, pp. 17, 61). The same is true for plates 120–24.
Source: Smithsonian Institution, Washington, D.C., inv. no. 69.112.4, 13·8 × 8·9 cm, mounted on paper, and inscribed below the print 'Moholy-Nagy '21'; on the verso, stamp 'L. Moholy-Nagy' and 'Berlin. W. 35/ Lützowstr. 73/IV'.

111 Photogram, 1922
Source: Levy Coll., described as 'postcard-photo board, 18·9 × 13·9 cm, verso, signed and dated 1922'.

112 Photogram, 1922
Source: Smithsonian Institution, Washington, D.C., described as '18 × 12 cm', mounted on paper and inscribed beneath print '1921' (for dating cf. note to pl. 110).

113 Photogram, n.d. (1922–23)
With this photogram Moholy broke away from the Constructivist emphasis on angles. The gradation of light produces a more spatial effect even if the material structures of his first attempts are still present. The total construction is in its forms reminiscent of a painting done by Rodchenko in 1920 (see figure).
Repr.: *Broom*, March 1923.
Source: Hug Coll.

114 Photogram, n.d. (about 1923)
Repr. LM-N, Photo-sculpture advertisement in *Offset*, 7, 1926, p. 389.
Source: *MFF* (1927), p. 74; English ed., p. 76.

115 Photogram, n.d. (1922?)
Repr.: *Das deutsche Lichtbild*, 1927, p. 116 (upright); LM-N, 'Abstract of an Artist' in *The New Vision*, 4th ed., 1949, p. 72, adapted as a montage and dated 1922. (According to Lucia Moholy the date of this photogram is earlier; however, it certainly did not exist as a montage in 1922.)
Source: *MPF* (1925), p. 66 (upright), and *MFF* (1927), p. 72 (landscape); also English ed., p. 74, with caption 'Organised effects of light and shade bring a new enrichment of our vision'.

116 Photogram, n.d. (1922–23)
Still related to pl. 113, but with a recognizable attempt to produce a complicated 'cubist' space.
Repr.: *MPF*, p. 65, and *MFF*, p. 71 (also English ed., p. 73), all landscape; Roh, no. 17 (upright), described as 'Geometrizing bright-dark structure'; *Photographische Korrespondenz*, 1927, p. 210 (upright, with the cross at the bottom); *Führer VDAV*, Berlin 1927, p. 18 (upright, with the cross at the bottom).
Source: *MFF*, p. 71.

117 Photogram, n.d. (1922–23)
According to a statement by Sibyl M-N, this photogram shows Moholy 'lighting a cigarette' (cf. Sibyl M-N, *Experiment in Totality*, 1969, fig. 12, with caption 'Moholy lighting a cigarette'). Lucia Moholy told me personally and in a letter that photographic technique could not show the flame of a match. According to her, the photogram shows the profile of the *Der Sturm* artist Rudolf Blümner, and this is valuable as proof of Moholy's

Pl. 113

A. Rodchenko, *Composition*, oil painting, 1922.

close personal contacts with Expressionist circles. According to Lucia Moholy, one would have to date this photogram before Moholy's time at the Bauhaus, i.e. about 1922–23.
Repr.: Sibyl M-N, *Experiment in Totality*, 1969, fig. 12.
Source: Hug Coll.; another example in GEH (8099, 37 × 27·5 cm) described as 'Self-portrait lighting a cigarette 1924'.

118 Photogram, n.d. (1924?)
This sheet belongs (like pls. 123, 124, 129, 130, 138, 146, 147) to a series of photograms which Moholy produced in an edition of twenty copies, size 40 × 30 cm. A print of this example was formerly in the possession of Theo van Doesburg.
Source: Basle, Kupferstichkabinett, inv. no. 1968.415.5, 40 × 30 cm.
Other examples in: Galleria Milano, described as 'photogram 1926, 40 × 30 cm, signed in ink on verso, with stamp "foto ex coll. Van Doesburg"'; also Städtische Kunsthalle, Mannheim, dated 1924.

119 Photogram (1922?)
The date 1922 on the Budapest print, which cannot be the original on account of its small size, is not improbable. Related to pl. 115.
Repr.: Sibyl M-N, *Experiment in Totality*, p. 72, dated 1926.
Source: Verband ungarischer Fotokünstler, Budapest, inv. no. 5822, described as '16·3 × 12 cm', verso inscribed 'Konstruktion 1922'; another example in GEH, dated 1926.

120 Photogram (1922?)
Repr.: Roh, no. 7, with caption 'Blitz durchlaufenes astrales Schimmern' (Astral shimmerings shot through with lightning).
Source: Gernsheim Coll., described as '23·3 × 17·8 cm', on the verso signed and dated 1922; another example in MOMA.

121 Photogram, n.d. (1926?)
Spiral-like rotation of space, comparable to pl. 118.
Source: Roh (title page).

122 Photogram, n.d.
Lucia Moholy suggests 1925–26 as the probable date.
Source: GEH, described as '40 × 47·8 cm, 1924'.

123 Photogram (1922?)
Source: Kunstgewerbemuseum, Zurich, inv. no. 1955–4f, described as 'signed and dated 1922', stamps 'a + b'; another example in the Ludwig Collection, Cologne, dated 1924.

124 Photogram (1923)
Repr.: *Telehor*, no. 44, as 'Fotogramm 1923'.
Source: Kunstgewerbemuseum, Zurich, inv. no. 1955–4b, described as 'signed and dated 1923', stamps 'a + b'.

125 Photogram (1925?)
A comparison with pl. 132 suggests that 1925 is more probable than Moholy's own (later) dating of 1922; Lucia Moholy suggests 1924–25.
Source: LM-N, *Vision in Motion*, 1947, fig. 240, with date 1922.

126 Photogram (1926)
Source: GEH, described as '23·9 × 17·9 cm, 1926'.

127 Photogram, n.d. (1925–29)
Comparable to pl. 133.
Repr.: LM-N, 'Photogram und Grenzgebiete' in *Die Form*, 10/1929, p. 256.
Source: Kunstbibliothek, Staatliche Museen, Stiftung Preußischer Kulturbesitz, Berlin (West), inv. no. 32.307.

Pl. 127

Moholy's hand with toy gyroscope ('virtual volume'); from LM-N, *Von M zu A*, p. 82.

128 Photogram, n.d. (1923–25)
In *Telehor* Moholy dated a comparable photogram (pl. 136) to 1923; Lucia Moholy suggests a later date, about 1924–25.
Source: Klihm Coll., 17·4 × 24 cm.

129 Photogram (1924–26)
Source: Kunstgewerbemuseum, Zurich, inv. no. 1955–4c, described as being signed by Moholy with, in another hand, 'Dessau 1926'; another example, Ludwig Coll., Cologne, dated 1924.

130 Photogram (1922?)
Even though the use of spirals is reminiscent of pl. 110, the date 1922 seems exceptionally early. Moholy used this photogram later, in 1931, as the basis for a carnival advertisement.
Source: Kunstgewerbemuseum, Zurich, inv. no. 1955–4a, described as 'signed and dated 1922'.

Pl. 130

L. Moholy-Nagy, graphic contribution to a series 'Carnivals in Berlin, Munich and on the Rhine' in *die neue linie*, January 1931.

131 Photogram (1925–27)
Comparable to pl. 132.
Source: Kupferstichkabinett, Basle, inv. no. 1968.417, Arp-Hagenbach Collection, 23·8 × 17·9 cm.

132 Photogram (1925–27)
Moholy reproduced this photogram in *Von M zu A* (1929), p. 89 (English ed., p. 39, with caption, 'Photographic surface treatment by light ... This is the recording of light as it hit a projection screen − in this case the sensitive layer of the photographic paper.').
Source: Levy Coll., inv. no. 1975.1142, described as '17·8 × 23·9 cm., signed and dated 1927'.

133 Photogram, n.d.
Source: GEH, 38·6 × 29·6 cm.

134 Photogram (positive), n.d. (after pl. 133)
The taking of good photographic positives is only possible by a double photographic procedure: (1) by exposure on a glass negative; (2) exposure of this glass negative on to a second negative which then possesses the distribution of brightness of the original photogram. The paper prints made from this second negative show as dark forms areas that were originally bright. Since we know that Moholy never mastered practical photographic techniques, we may assume, particularly in these cases, the active collaboration of an experienced photographer (in the 1920s, Lucia Moholy).
Source: GEH, 38·4 × 28·5 cm, with rubber-stamp signature (below, right) 'L. Moholy-Nagy'.

135 Photogram (positive), n.d. (after pl. 136)
Source: MOMA, inv. no. 490.39, described as '7 × 9½, pencil additions'.

136 Photogram, n.d. (1923–25)
For dating cf. pl. 128.
Repr.: W. Warstadt, 'Die "entfesselte Kamera" und die "produktive Photographie". Zu den Ideen Professor Moholy Nagys', in *Deutscher Kamera-Almanach*, 1929, p. 43; *Telehor*, no. 42, with date 1923; LM-N, 'fotografie ist lichtgestaltung', in *Bauhaus*, 1928, p. 3.
Source: LM-N, 'Neue Wege in der Photographie', in *Photographische Rundschau*, 1928, pp. 33–36, as 'Photogram 2' with caption 'In this photogram one can no longer recognize the means that have been employed. The effect results only from the organization of light or light-dark contrasts respectively by the use of reflecting and absorbing planes. This is the actual aim and constitutes the purity of photography without a camera: to achieve a forceful effect by purely photographic means.'

137 Photogram, n.d. (about 1925)
Repr.: Beaumont Newhall, *History of Photography,* 1964, p. 163, whose dating is given here.
Source: University Art Museum, University of New Mexico, Albuquerque (ex coll. Beaumont and Nancy Newhall), 23·8 × 17·9 cm.

138 Photogram, n.d. (about 1925)
An almost identical photogram in the Larson Collection is dated 1925 in Moholy's own hand.
Source: Kupferstichkabinett, Basle, inv. no. 1968.415.1, Arp-Hagenbach Collection, 40 × 30 cm.

139 Photogram (1922)
The photogram seems to have been produced at about the same time as pl. 117. The 'chin' is pasted over with a piece cut from another photogram.
Source: GEH, described as '37·4 × 27·4 cm. Self-portrait profile, 1922'.

140 Photogram, n.d. (1925–27)
The date of origin is probably close to that of pls. 125, 131 and 132. A similar hand photogram, in the Larson Coll., is dated 1926 in Moholy's own hand.
Repr.: LM-N, 'Neue Wege in der Photographie', in *Photographische Rundschau*, 1928, pp. 33–36, as 'Photogramm', LM-N, 'fotografie ist lichtgestaltung', in *Bauhaus*, 1928, p. 2. Both publications have the caption: 'The primitive form of the photogram which, however, is not the result of simply laying down the head and illuminating it: differently organized light sources were used in different phases. Particularly noticeable is the distribution of the brightest tone values.'
Source: Larson Coll., described as '24 × 17·8 cm', inscribed on the verso '182 Moholy-Nagy fotogramm keine retusche [no retouching]'.

141 Photogram (?), n.d. (1930?)
If this really is a photogram, the dark grid must have been produced by copying, despite the black background. However, it might be a camera photograph of projections on to different transparent planes. The superimposed

floating light planes are reminiscent of Moholy's stage designs on which he was actively engaged at the same time (cf. Sibyl M-N, *Experiment in Totality*, p. 56), as well as of the 'Light-Space-Modulator' (cf. pl. 107).
Source: Hug Coll.

142 Photogram (positive), n.d.
Here, the patterns of the structures correspond to those of photograms produced about 1922 (cf. pl. 119). On the other hand the forms are very similar to the treatment of shadows in the abstract film *Light Display, Black and White and Grey* which was produced in 1930 by means of the Light-Space-Modulator (cf. pl. 107).
Source: Bauhaus-Archiv, Berlin.

143 Photogram, n.d. (before 1928)
Source: LM-N, 'Neue Wege in der Photographie', in *Photographische Rundschau*, 1928, pp. 33–36, as 'Photogramm 1', with caption 'Photogram in which increased emphasis was put on the effect of form. Use has been made of wires, rods and patterns.'

144 Photogram (1926)
Source: Roh, no. 27, reproduced there with caption 'Fotogramm 1926'.

145 Photogram, n.d. (1923?)
It is certain that this photogram was produced in association with pls. 128, 135 and 136.
Repr.: *Telehor*, no. 41 (with date '1923'); LM-N, 'Das Photogramm', in *Das neue Frankfurt* 3, 1929, p. 80 (reversed); LM-N, 'Photographie ist Lichtgestaltung' (inverted) in *Photgraphiche Korrespondenz*, 1 May 1928, with the following remark in the text: 'It should be noted that camera-less photographs possess as negative prints a wonderful softness of grey tones flowing into each other; whilst positive prints (which can also be produced from paper negatives) result in harder, often pale grey tones. Their quite particular quality will be only gradually recognized'. The procedure of using paper negatives which is mentioned here must have been a kind of Talbotype, in which a paper print (the original photogram) is made transparent by means of gelatine or some similar material and is then copied by contact printing on to photographic paper. Such procedures were also recommended to amateurs in periodicals dealing with photography (cf. H. Reuter, 'Kameralose Photographie', in *Photospiegel*, supplement to the *Berliner Tageblatt*, no. 3, 1929). One might conclude from the slight 'graininess' of the surface that such a procedure was used for the production of this photogram, as well as for pls. 135 and 142. However, this process is excluded in the case of pl. 134 on the account of the flowing smooth grey surfaces seen there.
Source: Allan Frumkin Gallery, Chicago, described as '81 × 60 cm., Fotogramm "Der Spiegel" 1921 ex collection Dr. Frans Roh'. The date given – '1921' – is out of the question. The immense size shows that it must be a relatively late reproduction.

146 Photogram (positive), n.d. (1932?)
Repr.: *Telehor*, no. 37, dated 1923.
Source: Bauhaus-Archiv, Berlin, 39·7 × 30 cm, signed and numbered 1/20, with stamps 'a + b'.
Other examples: Kupferstichkabinett, Basle; Coll. Max Bill, Zurich, dated there '1924/25'.

147 Photogram, n.d. (1925)
Repr.: *Telehor*, no. 40, dated 1925.
Source: Kunstbibliothek, Staatliche Museen Stiftung Preußischer Kulturbesitz, Berlin (West), inv. no. 32.307.
Other examples: University Art Museum, University of New Mexico, Albuquerque, with personal dedication by Moholy: 'for Beaumont Newhall/L. Moholy-Nagy (1925/1936 London)'; Städtische Kunsthalle, Mannheim, dated 1924.

148 Photogram, n.d. (1926?)
Similar forms and the same utensils also appear in part in pls. 126 and 118.
Repr.: LM-N, 'Neue Wege in der Photographie' (a newspaper cutting from an unidentified journal of about 1925 in the archive of Dr Klihm), with the caption: 'a camera-less photograph in which the objects are still hardly recognizable. By the use of objects with different degrees of translucency and special lighting arrangements a picture resulted that looks somewhat like a Futurist painting.'
Source: MOMA, described as 'Fotogramm 1926 $9\frac{1}{4} \times 7$'.

149–150 Photogram (positive and negative), n.d. (1924)
A similar effect of forms appears in the 'Hyperboloid sculpture' by Joost Schmidt, which Moholy used as an illustration in *Von M zu A* (1929), p. 158 (English ed., p. 48). The sculpture is photographed in such a way as to resemble a photogram, floating on a black background, and follows, according to Moholy, 'the urge to take possession of the volume in its most sublime appearance'.
Source: *Telehor*, no. 36, dated '1924'.

THE PLATES

1   »bei mokka«, n. d.

2   Ascona, 1926

3   1926

4   Portrait Lucia Moholy, ca. 1926

5   Ascona 1926/La Sarraz, 1928

6   Portrait Lucia Moholy, Ascona, ca. 1926

7   1925

8 La Sarraz, 1928

9   La Sarraz, 1928–30

10   Stockholm, 1930

11   Helsinki, 1930

12   Marseille, 1929

13   Belle-Ile-en-Mer, 1925

14   Dessau, 1926—28

15   ca. 1925

16 Dessau, 1926–28

17 Lyon, ca. 1929

18 n. d.

19 Ascona, 1928

20　Belle-Ile-en-Mer, 1925

21 Berlin, ca. 1930

22 1929

23   Berlin, 1928

24   Dessau, 1926

25   Portrait Sibyl Moholy-Nagy, London, 1936

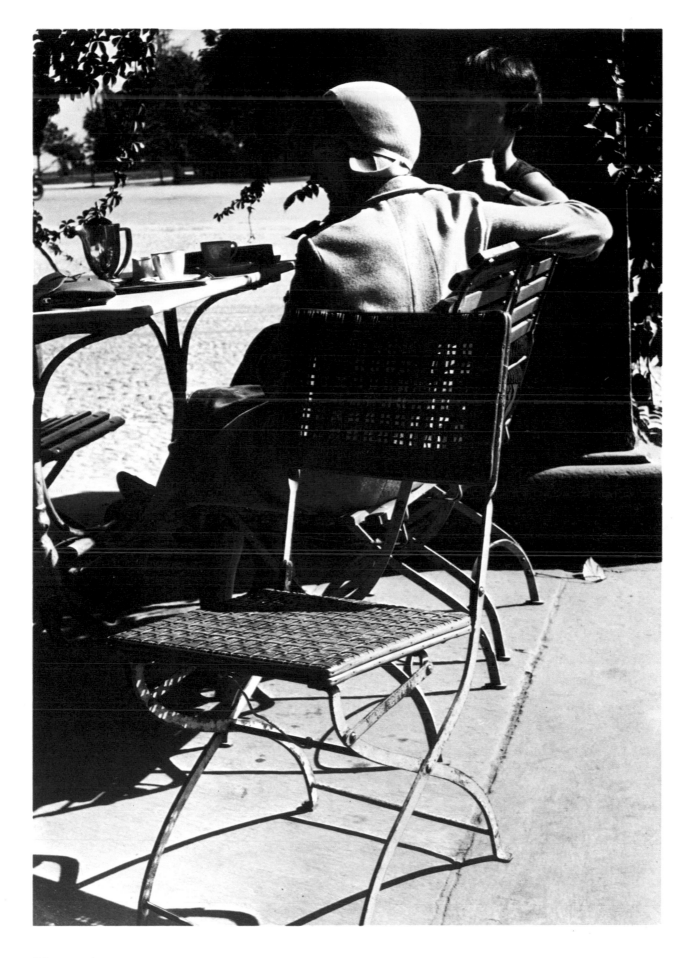

26 n. d.

27   Bexhill on Sea, 1936

28   Bexhill on Sea, 1936

29   Köln, 1920 (?)

30   Paris, 1925

31   Bagneux/Paris, 1925 (?)

32   Paris, 1925

33 Marseille, 1929

34   Paris, 1925

35 Zürich, 1920 (?)

36   Köln, 1927–29

37 Berlin, ca. 1928

38 Berlin, ca. 1928

39   Berlin, 1928

40　Berlin, 1928

41   Marseille, 1929

42   Marseille, 1929

43   Marseille, 1929

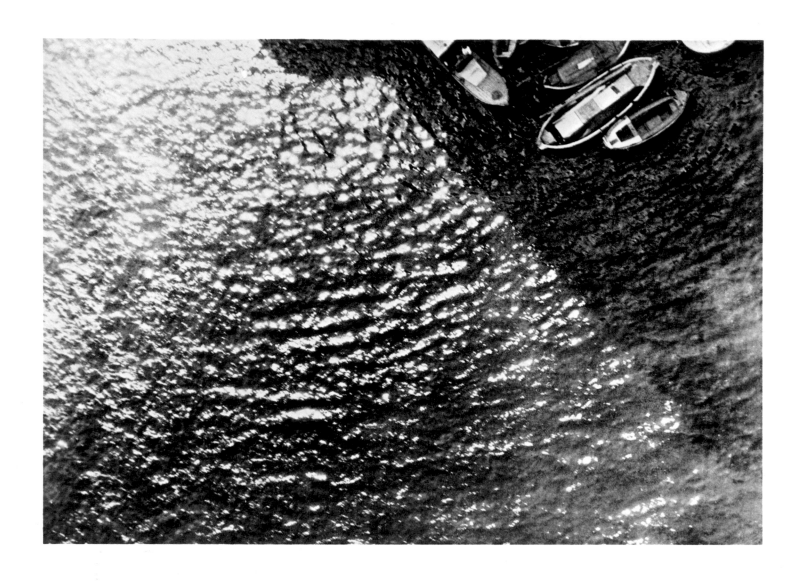

44   Marseille, 1929

45   Marseille, 1929

46   Marseille, 1929

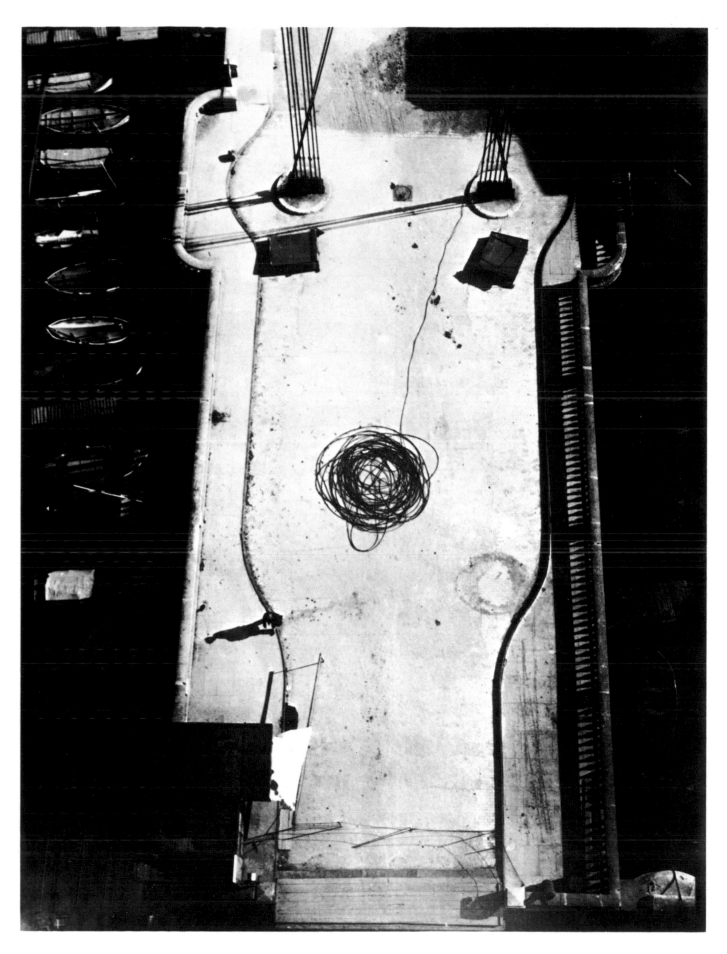

47 Marseille, 1929

48 Scandinavia, 1930

49   Scandinavia, 1930

50 Scandinavia, 1930

51   Scandinavia, 1930

52   Scandinavia, 1930

53　Scandinavia, 1930

54 Scandinavia, 1930

55   ca. 1927

56 Portrait Ellen Frank, ca. 1929

57 Portrait Vladimir Majakowski, 1924

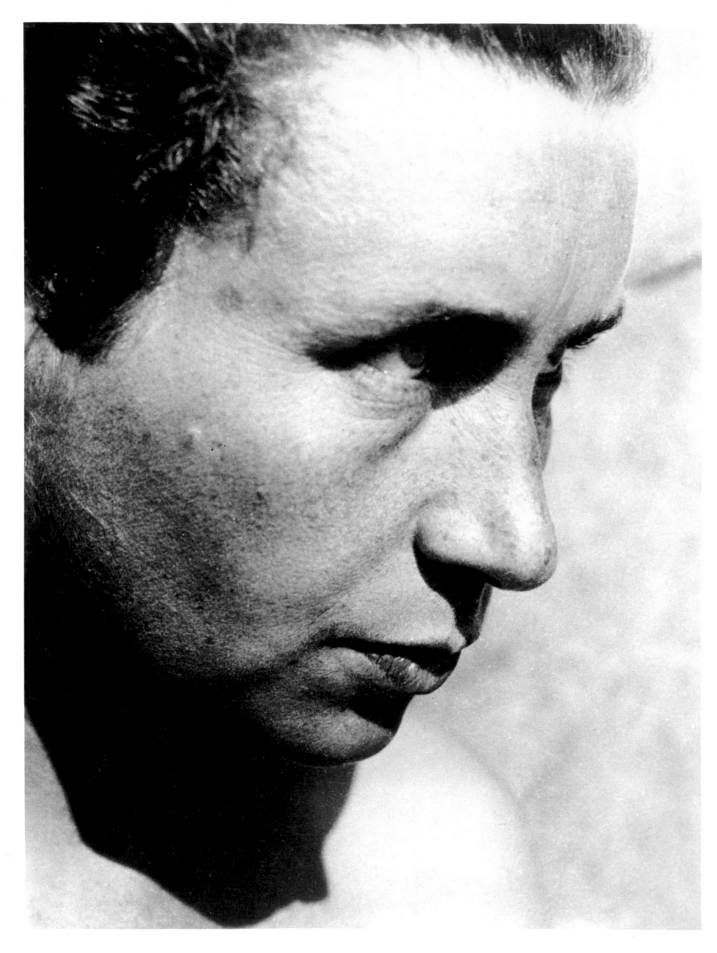

58   Portrait Lucia Moholy, 1924 (?)

59   Portrait

60 Portrait Lucia Moholy

61 Portrait Lucia Moholy

62   Portrait Solomon Guggenheim, ca. 1926

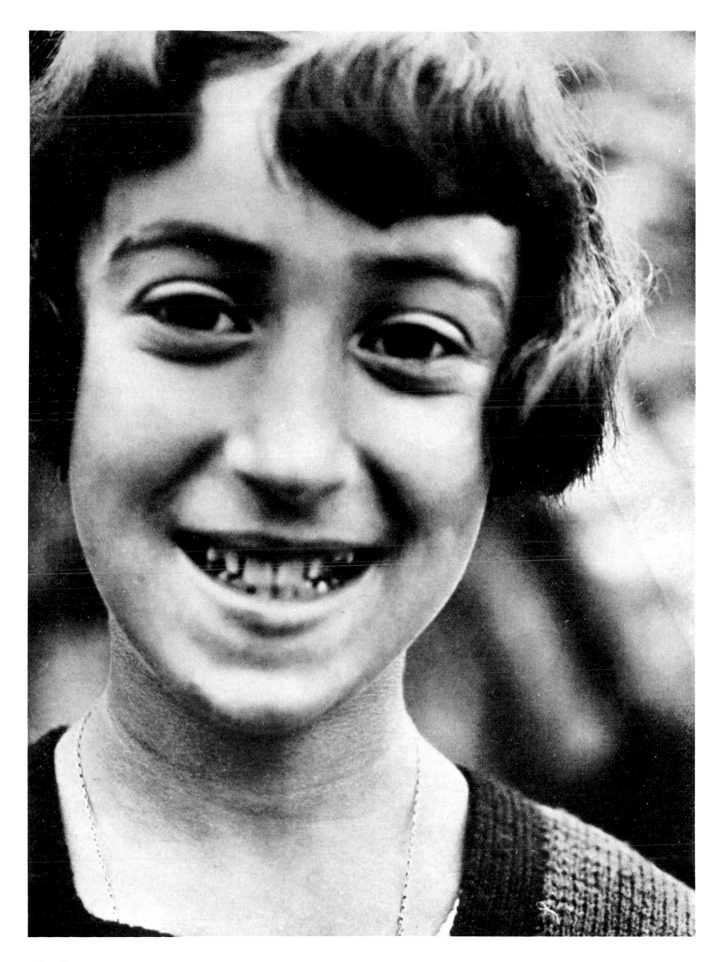

63 Portrait

64   Portrait

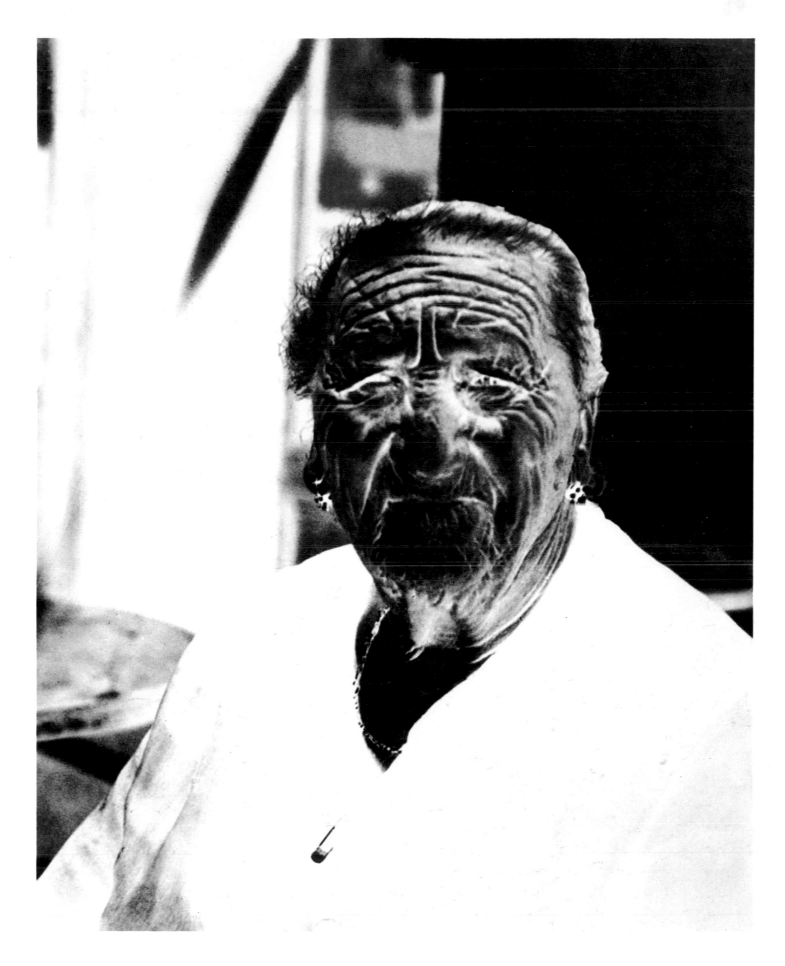

65 Portrait

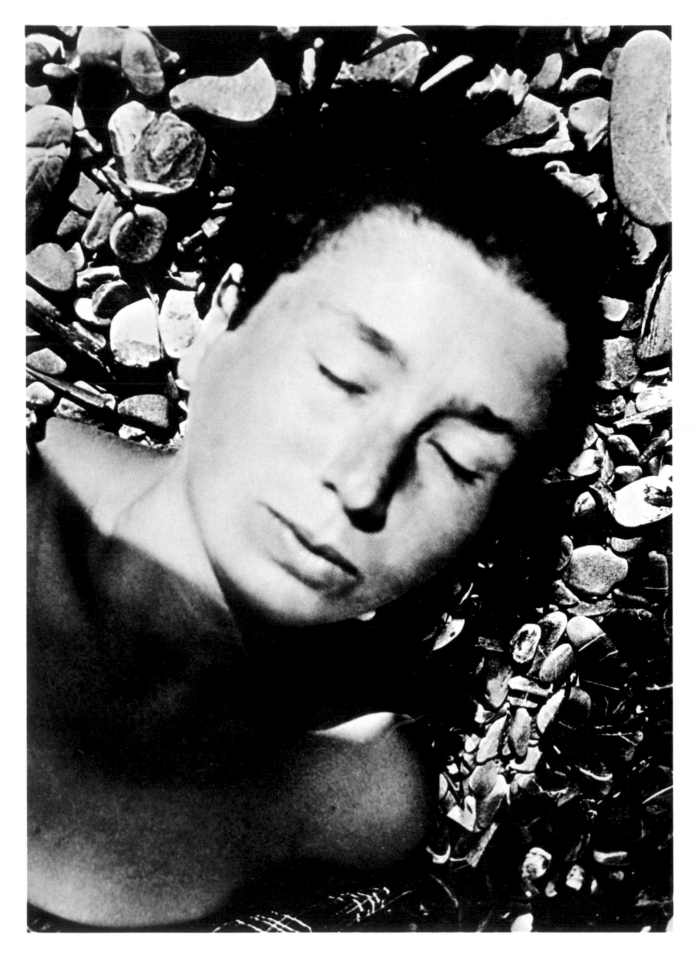

66   Portrait Lucia Moholy, 1925

67   Portrait

68   1927–29

69   1927—29

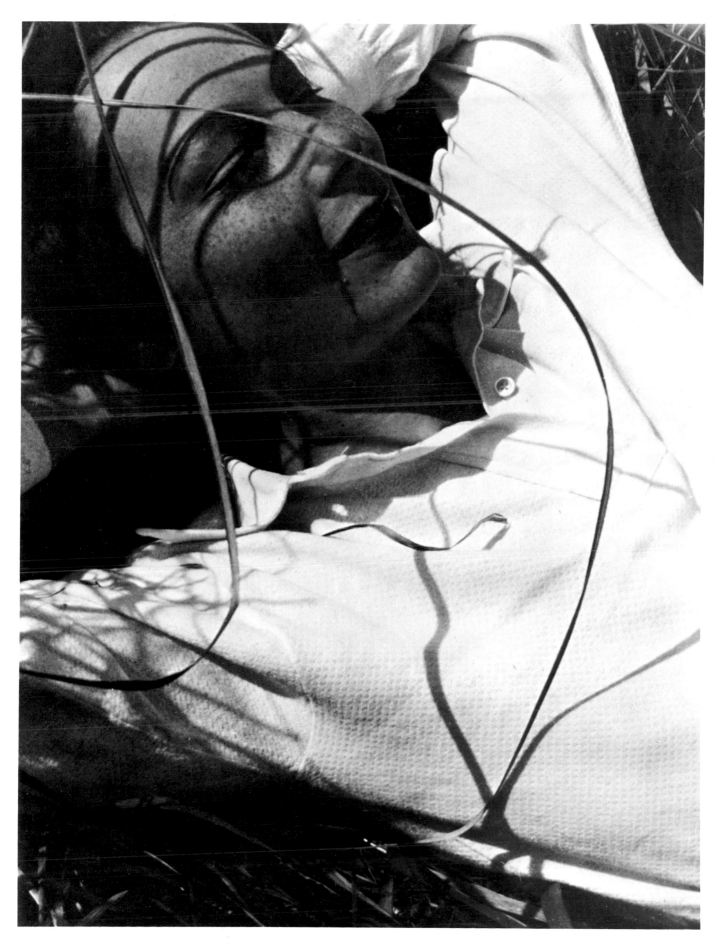

70   Portrait Ellen Frank, 1929

71   1927 (?)

72   1927

73   1931

74   1931

75 ca. 1929

76 Sellin, 1929

77   Sellin, 1929

78   1929 (?)

79   1929 (?)

80 1929 (?)

81   1930

82 1924 (?)

83 Ascona, 1926

84   1928

85   ca. 1926

86   Rhineland, 1923 (?)

87   Paris, 1925

88   Hiddensee, 1929 (?)

89 Belle-Ile-en-Mer, 1925

90   Marseille, 1929

91   Paris, 1925 (?)

92   Paris, 1925 (?)

93 Switzerland, 1925–30

94   1926 (?)

95   Paris, 1925 (?)

96 Marseille, 1929

97   Paris, 1925/Marseille, 1929

98   Berlin, 1932

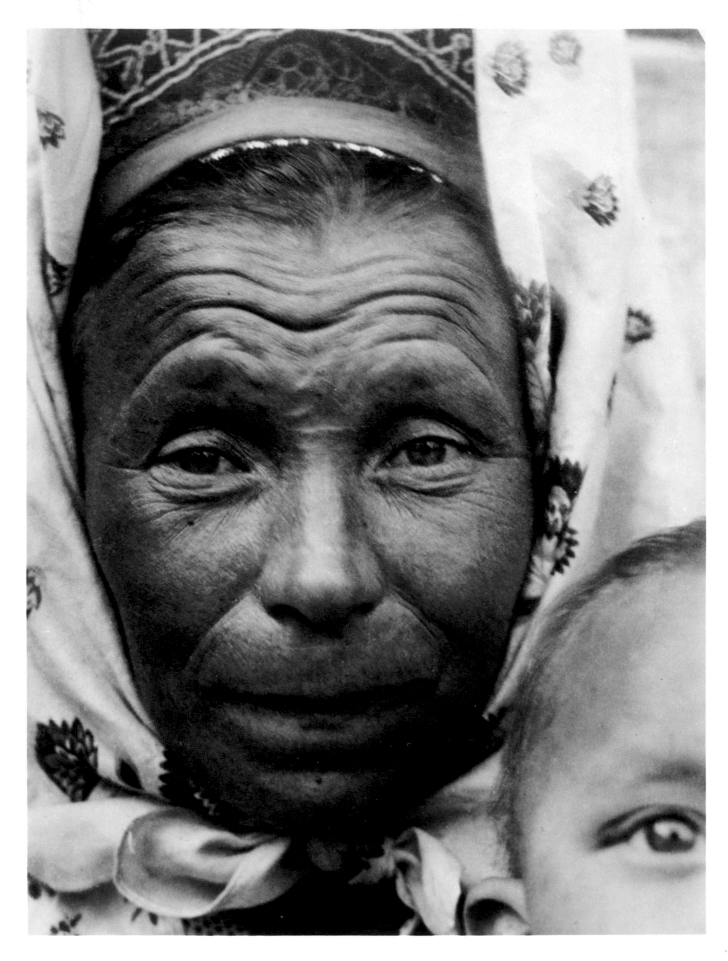

99 Portrait, 1930

100   Paris, 1925

101   Paris, 1925 (?)

102   London, 1935–37

103 Scandinavia, 1930

104   Marseille, 1929

105   1931 (?)

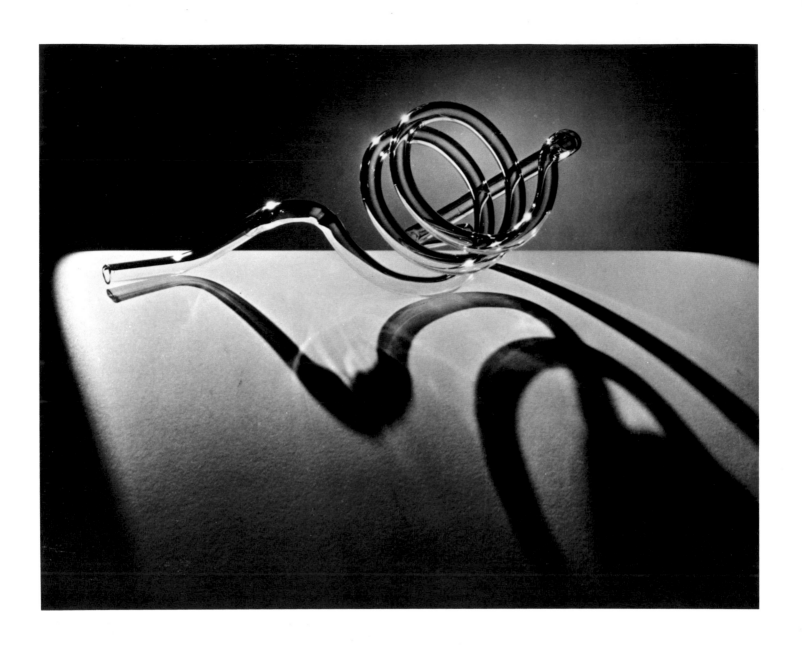

106   Chicago, 1938

107   1922–30

108   Fotogramm, 1922

109   Fotogramm, 1922

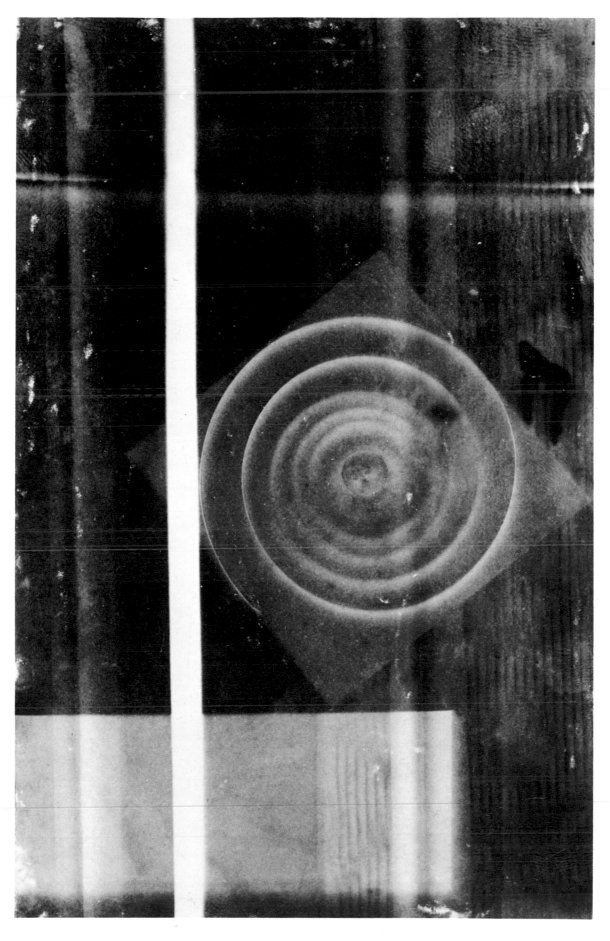

110   Fotogramm, 1922

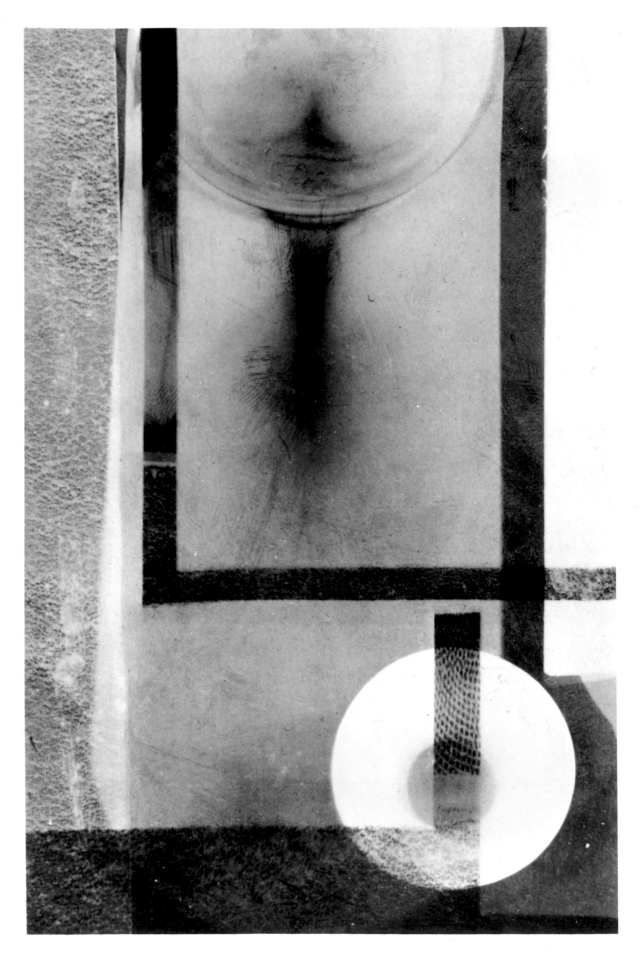

111   Fotogramm, 1922

112   Fotogramm, 1922

113   Fotogramm, 1922–23

114 Fotogramm, ca. 1923

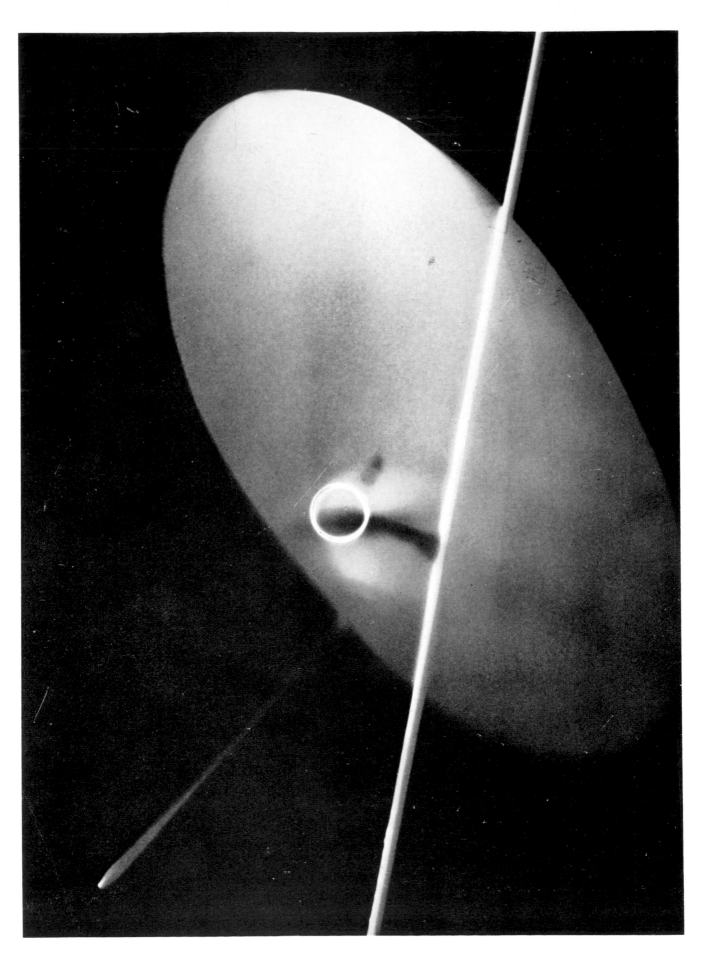

115   Fotogramm, 1922 (?)

116   Fotogramm, 1922–23

117   Fotogramm, 1922–23

118   Fotogramm, 1926 (?)

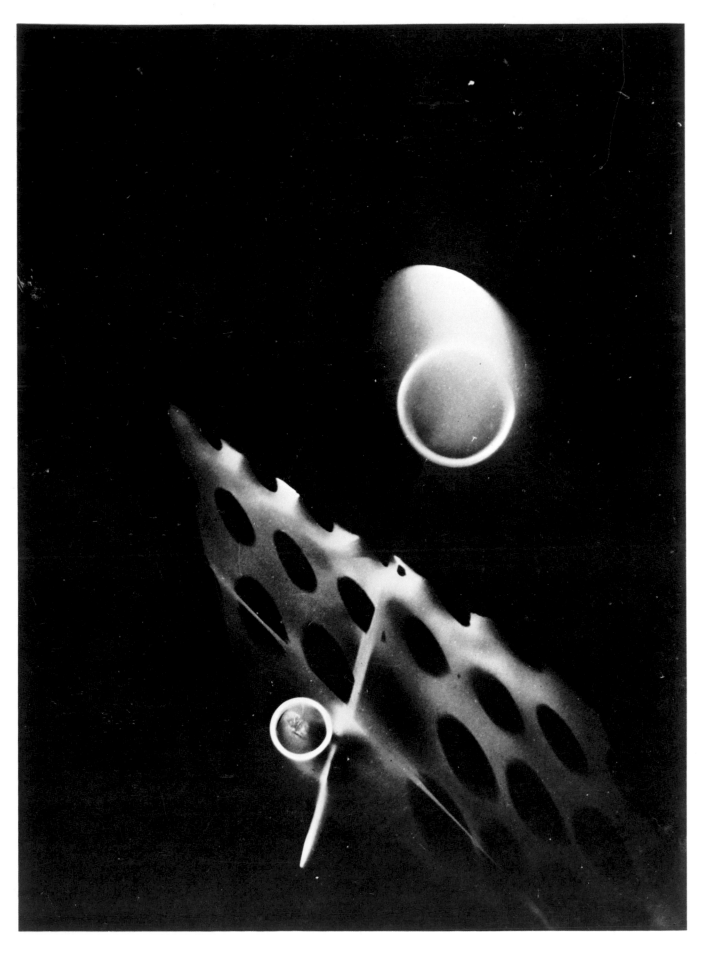

119　Fotogramm, 1922 (?)

120   Fotogramm, 1922 (?)

121   Fotogramm, 1926 (?)

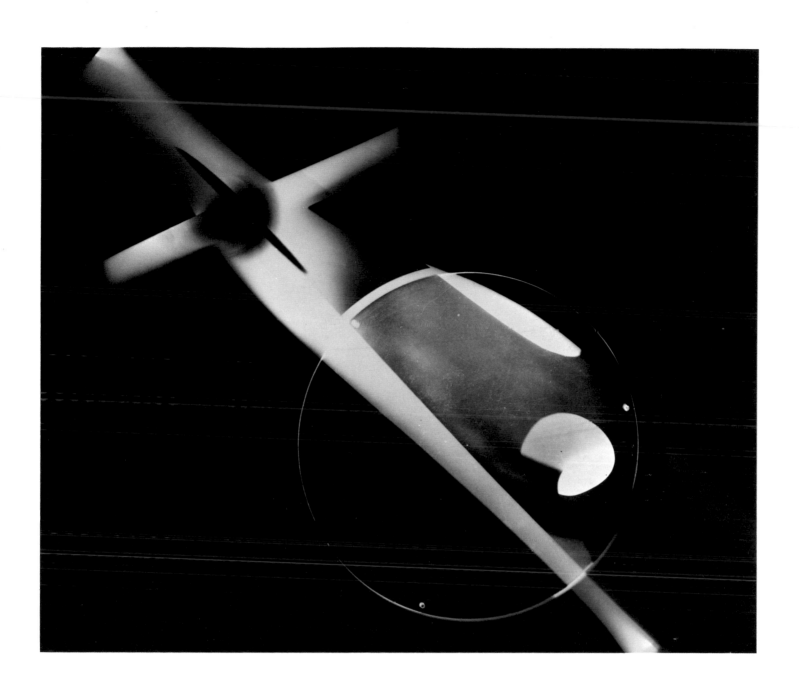

122 Fotogramm, 1924–29

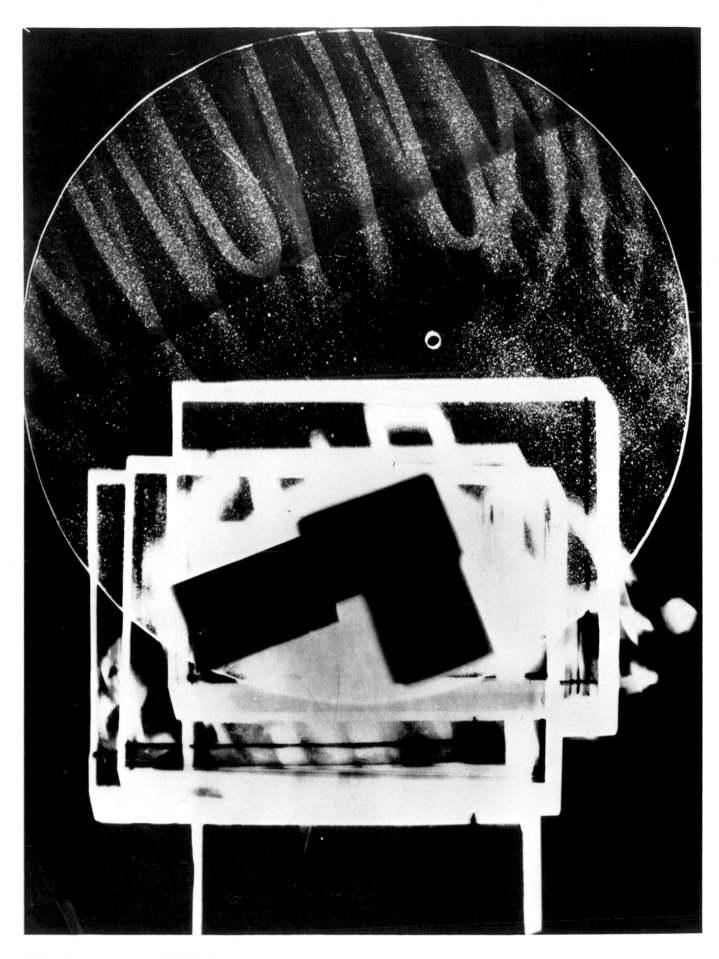

123   Fotogramm, 1922 (?)

124 Fotogramm, 1923

125   Fotogramm, 1925 (?)

126   Fotogramm, 1926

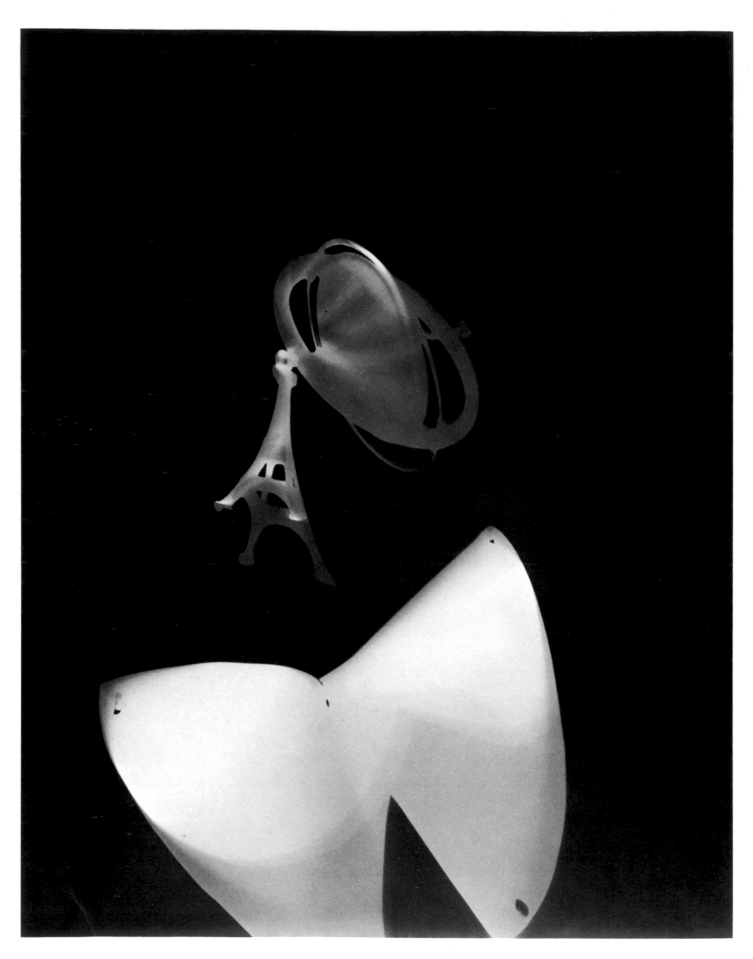

127   Fotogramm, 1925–29

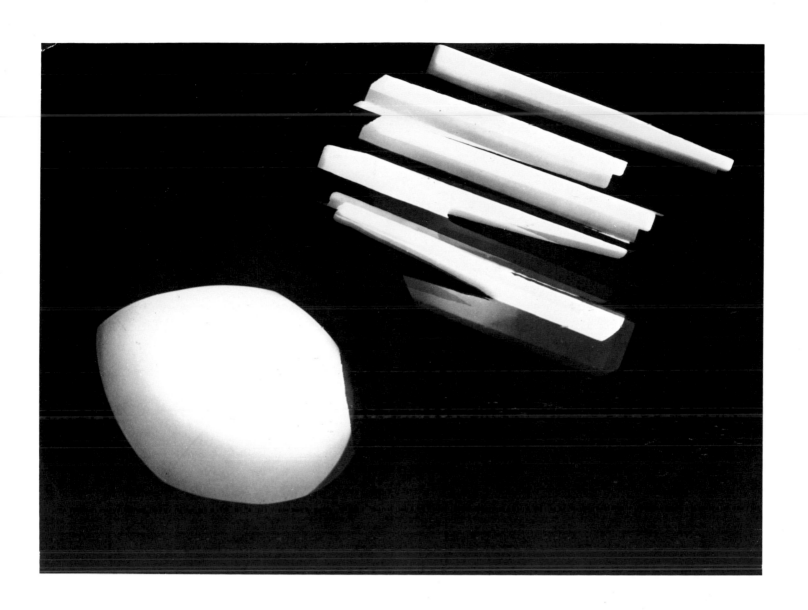

128   Fotogramm, 1923–25

129 Fotogramm, 1924–26

130   Fotogramm, 1922 (?)

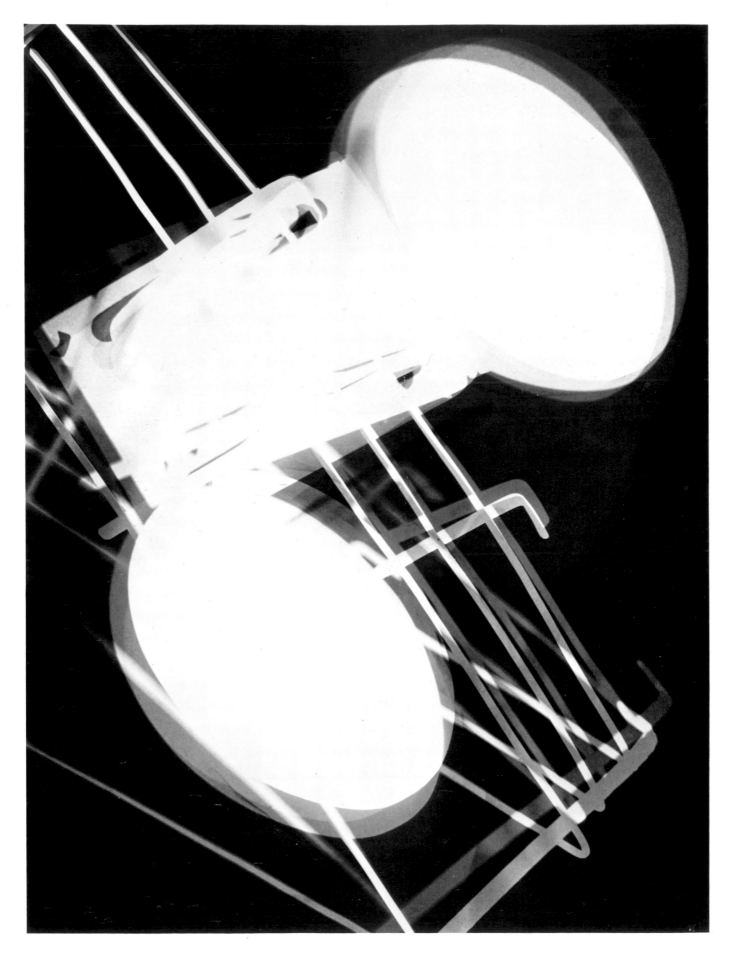

131   Fotogramm, 1925–27

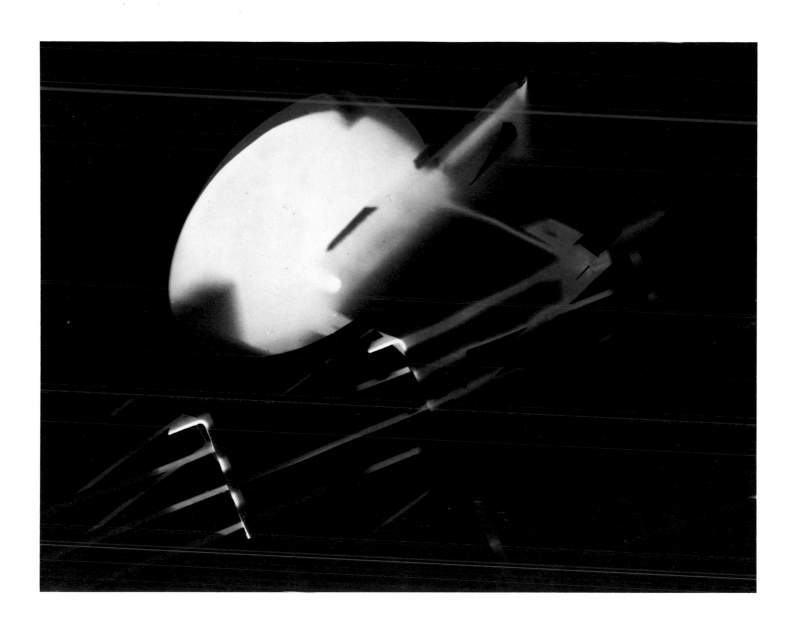

132 Fotogramm, 1925–27

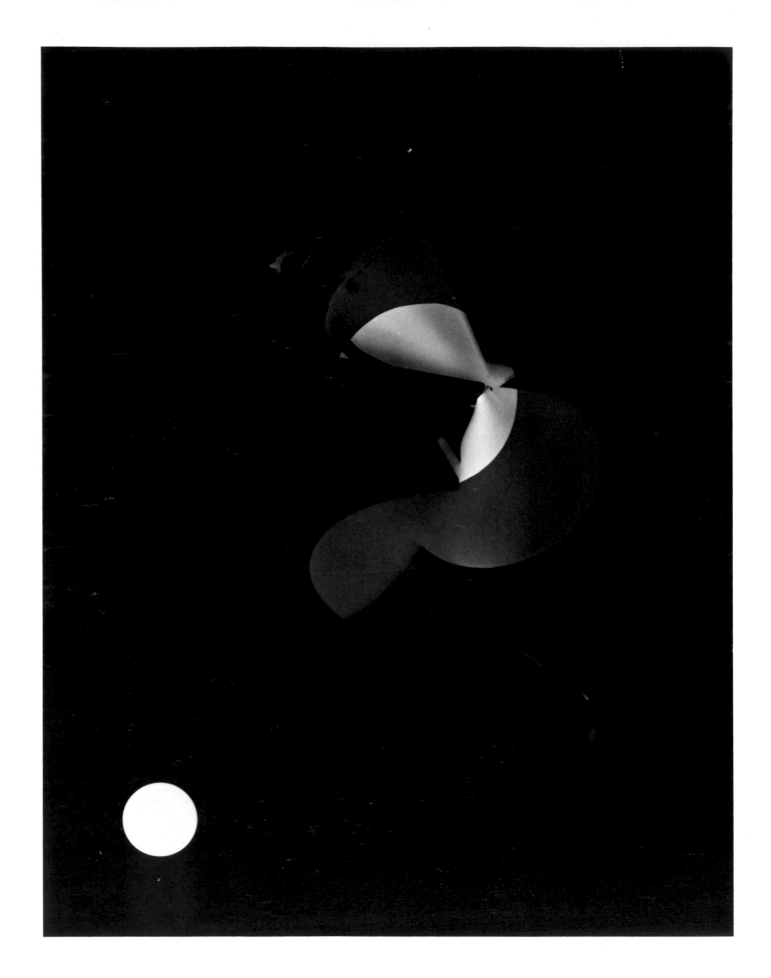

133 Fotogramm

134   Fotogramm, (pos.)

135 Fotogramm, (pos.)

136 Fotogramm, 1923–25

137   Fotogramm, ca. 1925

138   Fotogramm, ca. 1925

139   Fotogramm, 1922

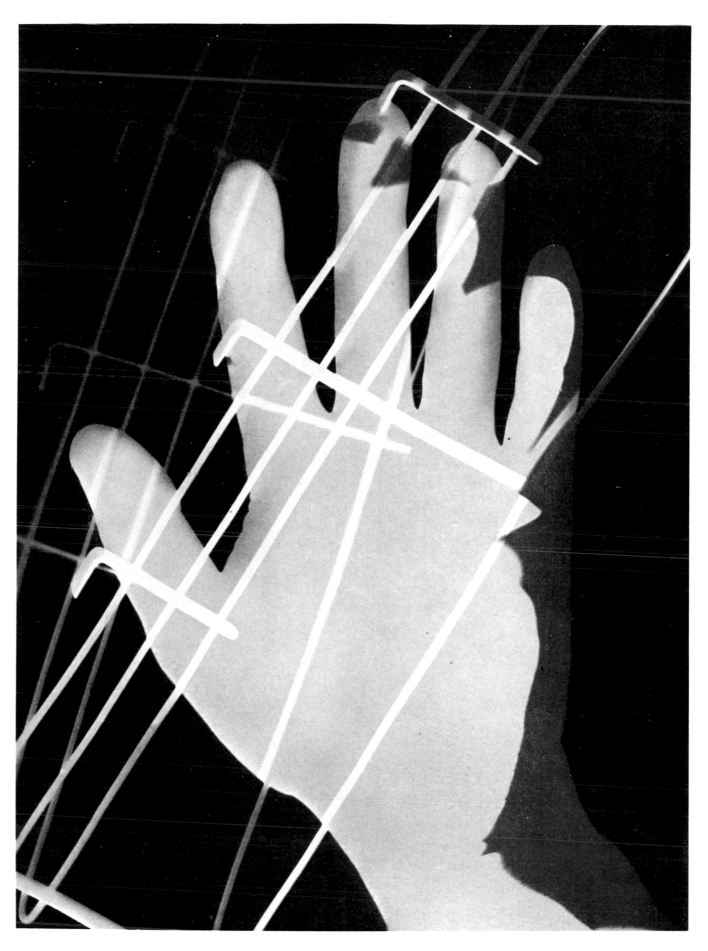

140   Fotogramm, 1925–27

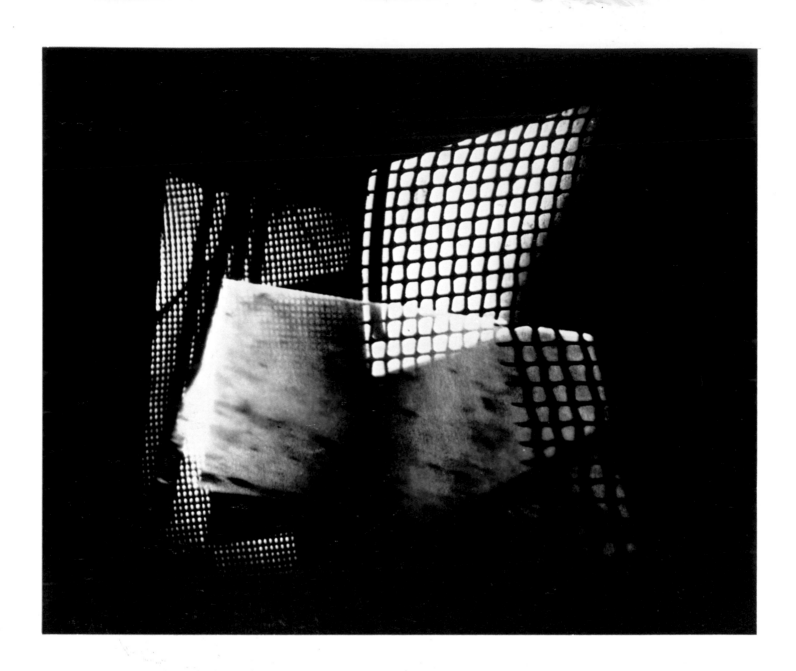

141   Fotogramm (?), 1930 (?)

142   Fotogramm (pos.)

143   Fotogramm, ca. 1928

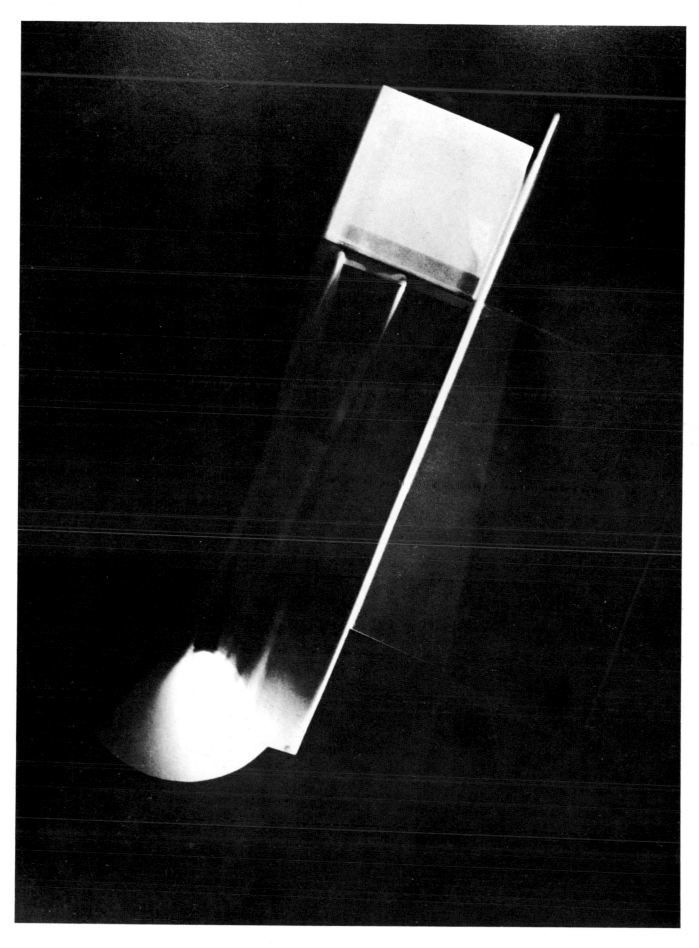

144   Fotogramm, 1926

145 Fotogramm, 1923 (?)

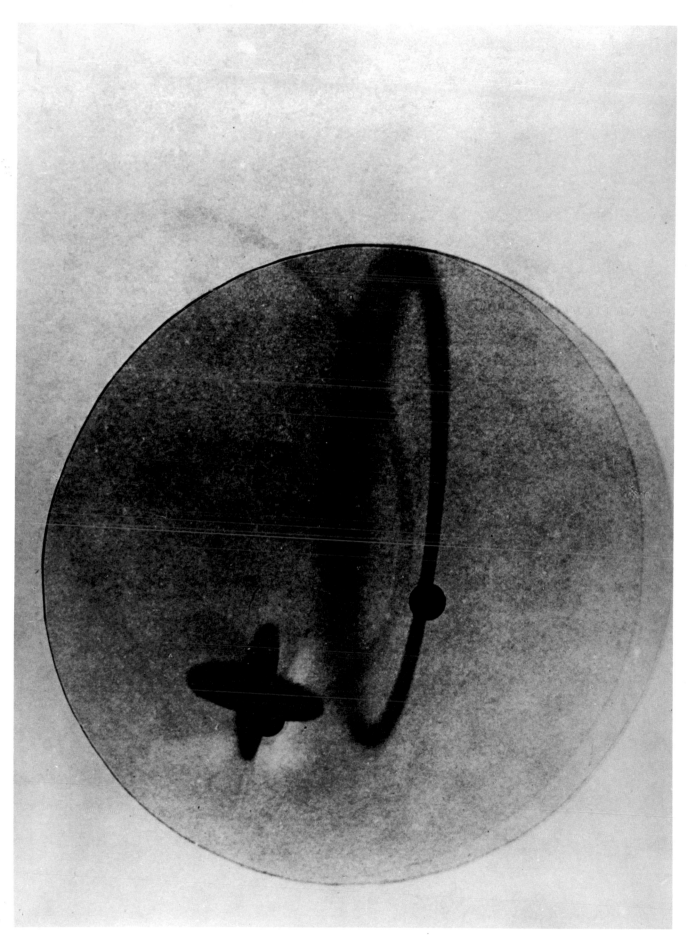

146 Fotogramm (pos.) 1923 (?)

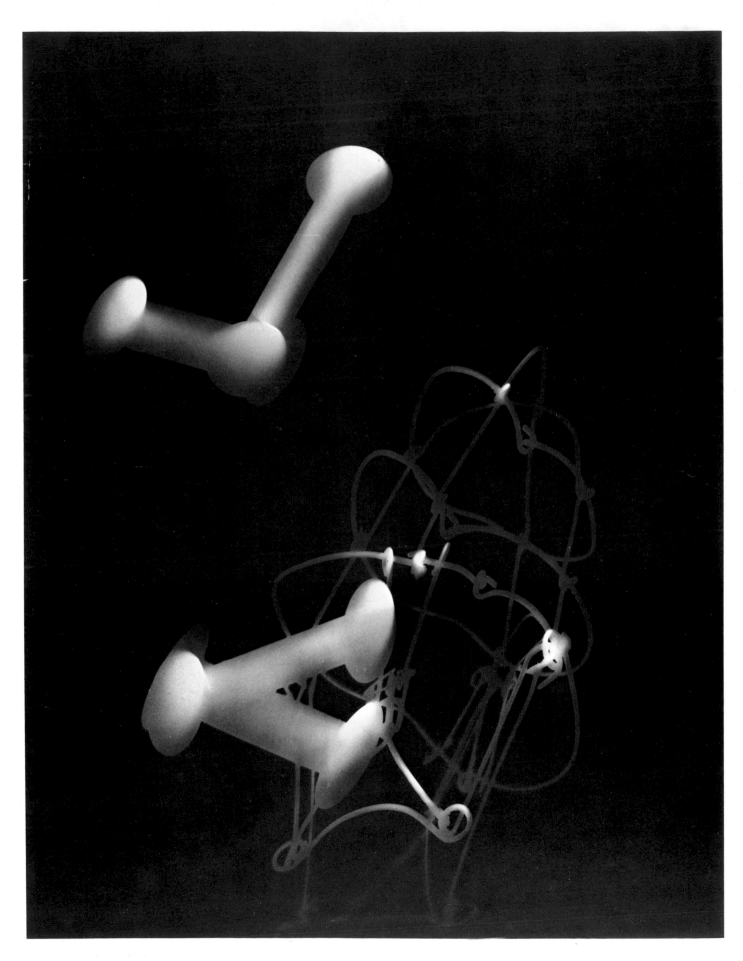

147   Fotogramm, 1925 (?)

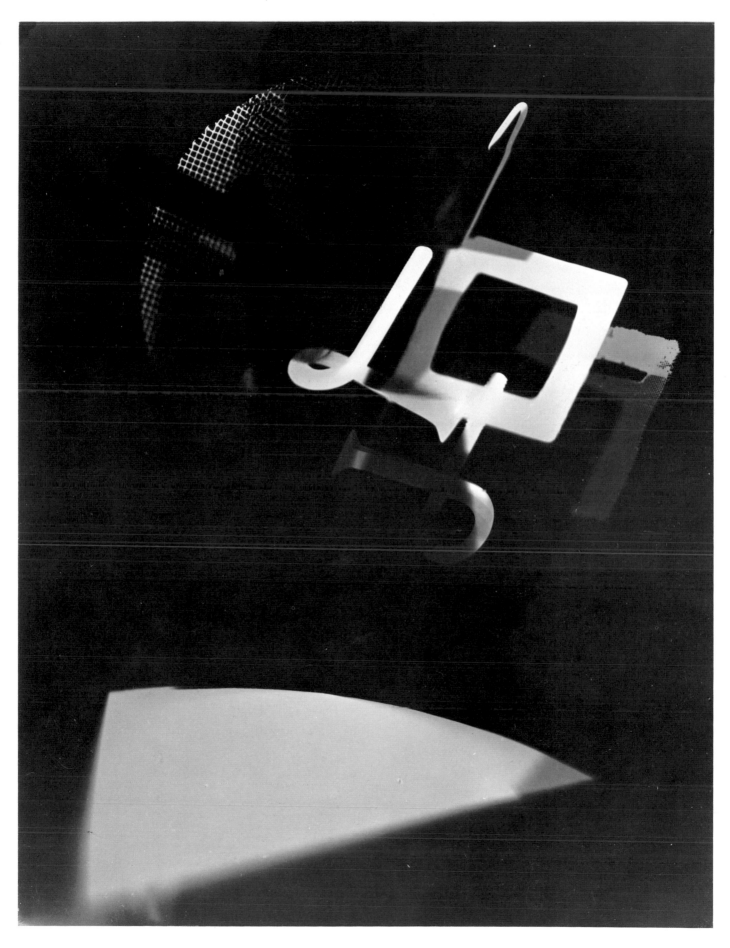

148   Fotogramm, 1926 (?)

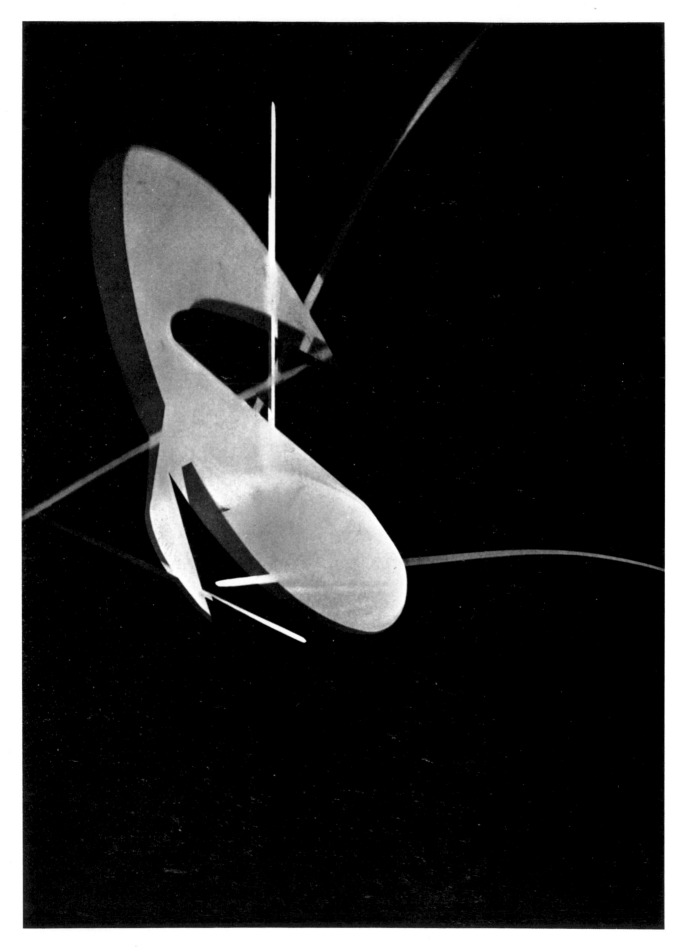

149   Fotogramm 1924

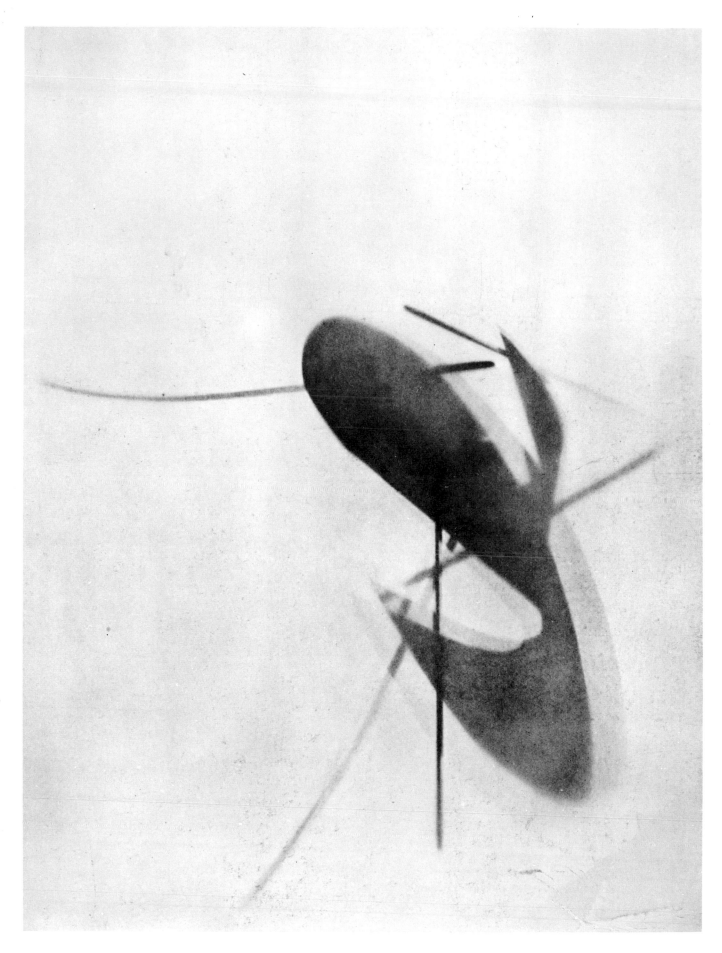

150 Fotogramm (pos.) 1924

far beyond the standard "headshot"

essence of subject
+ unique twist of insight

photo: phyllis christopher

PHYLLIS CHRISTOPHER

the black & white editorial portrait

exhibit june 20 through august 27

reception & refreshments july 24

photography ‖ observers, photographers & portrait subjects especially encouraged to attend

monday evening, 6:30 pm

berkeley public library   2090 kittredge at shattuck, downtown berkeley   info: 510-981-6100

central catalog lobby, first floor   mon & tues 12 - 8; wed-sat 10-6; sun 1 - 5

free   www.berkeleypubliclibrary.org   www.phyllischristopher.com   sponsored by the friends of the library

wheelchair accessible to request a sign language interpreter, real-time materials in large print or Braille or other accomodations, call 510-981-6107 or 510-548-1240 (TDD) by july 17th.
please refrain from wearing scented products to public meetings